Teaching Literacy Effectively in the Primary School

Teaching Literacy Effectively in the Primary School takes a close look at the characteristics of teachers who are known to be highly effective in their teaching of literacy. Using findings from a ground-breaking research study commissioned by the Teacher Training Agency, the authors uncover a number of distinctive features of these teachers in terms of their literacy teaching practices, their knowledge and beliefs about literacy and its teaching, and their experiences of professional development. The authors also consider these findings with regard to their implications for policy and practice.

This book makes a significant contribution to our understanding of the effective teaching of literacy, and of the qualities necessary in teachers if they are to provide it. It is essential reading for teachers in training, teachers in service and for those responsible for teacher professional development.

David Wray is Professor of Literacy at the University of Warwick. He has published over 40 books on literacy teaching, including *Literacy and Language in the Primary Years* and *Extending Literacy*, published by RoutledgeFalmer.

Jane Medwell is Director of the Primary PGCE programme and Lecturer in Literacy Education at the University of Warwick. She has researched and published widely in the area of literacy teaching.

Louise Poulson is Senior Lecturer in Education at the University of Bath.

Richard Fox was formerly Senior Lecturer in Primary Education at the University of Exeter.

Language and Literacy in Action Series
Series Editor: David Wray

Teaching Literacy Effectively in the Primary School
David Wray and Jane Medwell

Raising Standards in Literacy
Edited by Ros Fisher, Maureen Lewis and Greg Brooks

Teaching Literacy Effectively in the Primary School

David Wray, Jane Medwell,
Louise Poulson and Richard Fox

London and New York

First published 2002 by RoutledgeFalmer
11 New Fetter Lane, London EC4P 4EE

Simultaneously published in the USA and Canada
by RoutledgeFalmer
29 West 35th Street, New York, NY 10001

RoutledgeFalmer is an imprint of the Taylor & Francis Group

© 2002 David Wray, Jane Medwell, Louise Poulson and Richard Fox

Typeset in Sabon by BC Typesetting, Bristol
Printed and bound in Great Britain by University Press, Cambridge

British Library Cataloguing in Publication Data
A catalogue record for this book is available from the British Library

Library of Congress Cataloging in Publication Data
Wray, David
    Teaching literacy effectively in the primary school/David Wray
    and Jane Medwell.
       p.   cm. – (Language and literacy in action)
    Includes bibliographical references and index
    1. Language arts (Elementary)–Great Britain. 2. Reading
    (Elementary)–Great Britain. I. Medwell, Jane II. Title. III. Series.

    LB1576.W695 2001
    372.6'0941–dc21   2001019643

ISBN 0–415–23777–7 (pbk)
ISBN 0–415–23776–9 (hbk)

Contents

Tables

Acknowledgements

The research described in this book was undertaken with the support of the Teacher Training Agency (TTA), and we would like to acknowledge the help of a number of Frankie Sulke, formerly Head of Policy at the TTA, Philippa Cordingley, the Agency's Chief Research Adviser, and all the members of our Steering Committee. Many other people contributed to this researh, in particular, Alison Marchbank and Laurel Edmunds who undertook fieldwork, data coding and analysis; and Rachel Fitzroy who helped with administration of the project. We are also grateful to the NFER and Ralph Tabberer for allowing us access to a briefing paper on research into teaching, which informed Chapter 1 of this book; to Christine Agambar of OFSTED for advice and briefing on using OFSTED data; and to the LEA advisers and inspectors who helped us identify the effective teachers of literacy.

We would also like to acknowledge the previous publication of some of the material in the book in the following journals: Journal of In-service Education, Reading, Educational Review and Education 3–13.

The research would have of course been impossible without the generous contribution of all the teachers and schools involved. We were immensely privileged to visit the classrooms of so many talented teachers and the memories of those visits will remain with us for a long time. It goes without saying that any of the faults that there will inevitably be in our reporting of the research, and the implications we draw from it, are ours alone.

Series Editor's Preface

David Wray

There can be few areas of educational endeavour which have been more controversial than that of teaching literacy. Perhaps because, in an increasingly information-dense society, the ability to make sense of and to produce text is self-evidently crucial to success, even survival, literacy has assumed the major burden as a litmus test of 'educatedness'. With such a critical role in the process of becoming educated, it is inevitable that there will continue to be major debates about exactly what it means to be literate, and about how such a state might most effectively be brought about – that is, how literacy is taught. A proportion of the energy behind such debates has come from the diverse findings of research into processes and pedagogy. Yet much of the debate, especially in the popular media, has lacked a close reference to research findings and has focused instead on somewhat emotional reactions and prejudices.

Students of literacy and literacy education who want to move beyond the superficiality of mass media debates need access to reports and discussions of key research findings. There is plenty such material, yet it tends to suffer from two major problems. Firstly, it can be rather difficult to locate as it has tended to be published in a diverse range of academic journals, papers and monographs. Secondly, research reports are usually written for an academic audience and make great demands on practitioners and others who wish to understand what the practical classroom implications are of what the research reports.

It is to address both these problems, but especially the latter, that this series has been developed. The books in the series deal with aspects of the teaching of literacy and languages in a variety of educational settings. The main feature of all the contributing volumes is to provide a research-grounded background for teaching action in literacy and language. The books either, therefore, provide a review of existing research and theory, or an account of original research, in an area, together with a clear résumé and/or set of suggestions as to how this background might influence the teaching of this area. The series acts therefore as a bridge between academic research books and practical teaching handbooks.

Teaching literacy effectively

The first volume in the series exemplifies its philosophy. It reports a major research project exploring the characteristics of effective teachers of literacy. The aims of this research were to:

1 identify the key factors in what effective teachers know, understand and do which enable them to put effective teaching of literacy into practice in the primary phase;
2 identify the strategies which would enable those factors to be more widely applied;
3 examine aspects of continuing professional development which contribute to the development of effective teachers of literacy.

The book gives an account of the background, methods and findings of this project, but is concerned throughout to discuss what the findings of this project mean for teachers, headteachers and policy makers. It will, therefore, find a ready readership among classroom practitioners and school leaders.

David Wray
University of Warwick
August 2001

Introduction

Teaching literacy effectively:
an overview

Introduction

Given the powerful role of literacy in society, it is inevitable that standards of literacy and definitions of what constitutes 'being literate' should be a concern for educators. With the development of more and more uses and functions for literacy, it is certainly the case that children need to achieve ever higher standards of literacy to 'be literate' in their society. One major factor in raising standards must be the quality of the teaching of literacy that children experience, particularly during the primary phase of schooling.

High-quality literacy teaching demands high-quality literacy teachers, and any education system must attempt to maximise the expertise of teachers in teaching literacy. In order to direct improvements in the selection, training and professional development of teachers of literacy most profitably, a great deal can be learned from a study of those primary school teachers identified as effective in the teaching of literacy.

Such a study was the aim of the research described in this book. This research project was commissioned by the Teacher Training Agency with the aim of understanding more clearly how effective teachers help children to become literate. The research study involved a close examination of the work of a sample of teachers whose pupils were making effective learning gains in literacy. We also compared the work of these effective teachers with that of a more random sample of teachers whose pupils were making less progress in literacy. The book gives an account of the project, its main findings and their implications for policy and practice, as well as relating the outcomes to insights gained from other research and commentary.

Defining literacy

In order to begin a study of effective teachers of literacy, we first needed to be clear about what we actually meant by literacy. This, of course, can and has been defined very widely. For our purposes, literacy was seen as a unitary process with two complementary aspects, reading and writing. Seeing reading and writing in this way, simply as opposite faces of the same coin, emphasised a basic principle in the National Curriculum for English (DES, 1995); that is, the need to develop children's skills within an integrated programme and to interrelate the requirements of the Range, Key Skills, and Standard English and Language Study sections of the Programmes of Study.

In the documentation underpinning the National Literacy Strategy (DfEE, 1998), literacy was defined through an analysis of what literate children should be able to do. This produced the following list of statements.

> Literate children should:
> - read and write with confidence, fluency and understanding;
> - be interested in books, read with enjoyment and evaluate and justify their preferences;
> - know and understand a range of genres in fiction and poetry, and understand and be familiar with some of the ways that narratives are structured through basic literary ideas of setting, character and plot;
> - understand and be able to use a range of non-fiction texts;
> - be able to orchestrate a full range of reading cues (phonic, graphic, syntactic, contextual) to monitor and self-correct their own reading;
> - plan, draft, revise and edit their own writing;
> - have an interest in words and word meanings, and a growing vocabulary;
> - understand the sound and spelling system and use this to read and spell accurately;
> - have fluent and legible handwriting.

There were, in this analysis, three strands to the experiences that children needed in order to develop these competencies:

1   **word-level work**: i.e. phonics, spelling and vocabulary;
2   **sentence-level work**: i.e. grammar and punctuation;
3   **text-level work**: i.e. comprehension and composition.

The term 'level' was used here to refer to structural/organisational layers in texts. Each of these levels was seen as essential to effective reading and writing, and there was felt to be a very close interrelationship between them. At different stages of learning literacy, however, some levels, it was thought, would assume greater prominence in teaching. Word-level work might, for example, be much more to the fore in the beginning stages of literacy learning, even though teachers would also want to enable pupils to locate such work in the experience of meaningful texts rather than pursuing it as an end in itself.

The aims of the research

The aims of this research were to:

- identify the key factors of what effective teachers know, understand and do that enables them to put effective teaching of literacy into practice in the primary phase;
- identify the strategies that would enable those factors to be more widely applied;
- examine aspects of continuing professional development that contribute to the development of effective teachers of literacy.

The research was designed to answer these questions by gathering evidence in a number of ways:

- a questionnaire survey of the qualifications, experience, reported beliefs, practices and preferences in teaching literacy of a group of 228 teachers identified by the research team as effective in the teaching of literacy on the basis of a range of data, including pupil learning gains;
- observations of literacy lessons given by twenty-six of these effective teachers of literacy;
- interviews with these twenty-six teachers about the content, structure and organisation of the lessons observed and about the knowledge underpinning them;
- a 'quiz' designed to test teachers' subject knowledge about literacy.

Both quantitative data and qualitative data were collected to build up as full a picture as possible of the knowledge, beliefs and teaching practices of a group of teachers identified as effective at teaching literacy. For comparison purposes, similar data was also collected from a sample of 'ordinary' teachers (referred to as the validation group).

Full details about the research methods used are given in Chapter 2, and background details of the teachers involved can be found in Appendix A.

Research hypotheses

From a review of the existing research literature on effective teachers in general and effective teachers of literacy in particular, a number of specific hypotheses were generated, which our research then set out to test. From this review, three key areas emerged. Effective teachers appeared to:

1   systematically employ a range of teaching methods, materials and class-room tasks matched to the needs of the specific children they are teaching;

2   have coherent beliefs about the teaching of their subject;
3   have a well-developed knowledge of the subject and its pedagogical principles, which underpins their teaching.

A crucial point to make here is that, in the majority of areas, research had not yet demonstrated that these features were characteristic of effective teachers of *literacy*. However, we hypothesised that our research would suggest this to be the case and, therefore, we extrapolated from the general research on effective teachers, and from our own extensive knowledge of the field of literacy, to develop a number of specific hypotheses.

Methods of teaching

The literature on effective teaching in literacy suggests that there are several teaching techniques that appear to be linked with pupil progress in reading and writing. Our hypothesis was that effective teachers of literacy were likely to employ such techniques in a strategic way; that is, with a very clear purpose linked to the identified literacy needs of specific pupils. The teaching techniques we expected to find being employed included the following:

1   The deliberate teaching of the codes of written language. Such teaching was, we felt, most likely to be systematic, i.e. planned rather than simply *ad hoc*. 'Codes' here referred to textual features at word, sentence and text levels, and included:
    • sound–symbol correspondences, e.g. the most usual pronunciations of letters and letter groupings, letter recognition;
    • word features and their structures, e.g. syllables, prefixes, suffixes, inflections;
    • spelling patterns, e.g. *ight, ei* (as in *weir, their, weigh*);
    • vocabulary and word study, e.g. looking at synonyms, exploring word origins, vocabulary broadening;
    • punctuation, e.g. the effects of punctuation signs such as commas and question marks on text meaning;
    • grammatical constructions, e.g. subject–verb agreement, conjunctions;
    • text structures, e.g. narrative elements such as plot, setting, character; expository text features such as argument structure.
2   The creation of 'literate environments' that enhanced children's understandings of the functions of literacy and gave opportunities for regular and sustained practice of literacy skills, e.g. encouraging children to write for a range of audiences, provision of literacy materials in dramatic play areas, use of labels and notices to draw children's attention to the use of literacy, etc.
3   The provision of a range of models and examples of effective literacy practices, either provided by the teacher him/herself, for example by

demonstrating writing, including revision and drafting, or provided by displays of successful literacy outcomes and skill use, either from children's own work or from published materials.

4 The use of praise and constructive criticism in response to children's literacy work with a view to consolidating success, correcting errors and promoting growth.

5 The design and provision of focused tasks with academic content that would engage children's full attention and enthusiasm and was appropriate to their ages and abilities.

6 The continuous monitoring of children's progress through the tasks provided and the use of informal assessment to give a basis for teaching and reporting on this progress.

Belief systems

Teacher beliefs are theorised as being an important element of effective teaching. However, the literature is weak in terms of evidence about the ways beliefs link to practice, especially in the teaching of literacy. We therefore deliberately set out to investigate this linkage, and our working hypothesis was that effective teachers of literacy would have a coherent set of beliefs about the nature and the learning of literacy that played a guiding role in their selection of teaching approaches.

An example of beliefs not synchronising with teaching practice can be found in the writing lesson in which the teacher stresses to the children that the outcome should be 'an exciting story, with plenty of action and good ideas' but then proceeds in his/her reactions to their writing to emphasise exclusively the need for accuracy in spelling and presentation without reference to the declared criteria of excitement, action and good ideas. Such writing lessons are, according to the literature, not uncommon in primary schools, and most children learn very quickly to put their efforts into what their teacher *really* wants from the writing. However, we hypothesised that this dissonance between a teacher's reported beliefs about what he/she was aiming for in teaching and the real criteria for the task was less than effective in terms of children's progress. Beliefs and action that were consonant were more likely, we hypothesised, to promote such progress.

Subject knowledge

There is evidence that effective teachers of other subjects tend to possess a well-developed knowledge base in those subjects. Such a knowledge base appears to consist of knowledge about content, knowledge about children and their learning and knowledge about how to teach the subject effectively. However, it had not yet been established that effective teachers of literacy were in a similar position with regard to their 'subject'. We hypothesised that there would be a link between effective teaching of literacy and subject knowledge.

In defining subject knowledge in literacy, we were forced to extrapolate from more general studies of subject knowledge and we used a three-part model to guide our research. Subject knowledge, we felt, consisted of:

1 Knowledge of content, i.e. what is it that children need to learn in literacy in order to be counted as successful?
2 Knowledge about effective pedagogy, i.e. what are the accepted principles underlying the teaching of literacy, e.g. the sequence of teaching, the contexts in which literacy might best be learned?
3 Knowledge about learners and how they learn and knowledge of the particular children in their class, i.e. how do children learn to read, write and use language effectively and what are the capabilities of the children in their classes?

The most problematic of the above was content knowledge. Defining this was complex, largely because content in literacy covers both knowledge (e.g. knowledge of literature, knowledge of the linguistic system) and skills. Literacy teachers teach children *about* reading and writing and *how to* read and write. Success in literacy is measured not by what children know about texts, print, etc. but by what they can do with these.

Literacy skills are, and should be, taught directly. It is well documented, however, that learners have difficulty in transferring their skills to alternative contexts, and in literacy this transfer can only be tested and observed in settings other than those in which the literacy skills were taught. To enable this essential transfer of skills in literacy, learners need to be given plenty of guided opportunities to put their literacy into practice. Content knowledge in literacy had, therefore, also to include knowledge of the ways in which reading and writing were used as tools for learning.

The relationship between content knowledge and pedagogical knowledge also seemed to be complicated in literacy. Some content knowledge is essential for learners of literacy but some may be essential for teachers, yet not directly useful in effective literacy performance. Linguistic terminology is an example of this. Although it is true that children need to know some linguistic terms, such as 'sentence' and 'word', there is little evidence that children's reading or writing is improved by explicit knowledge of such terminology as 'predicate' or 'subordinate clause'. Yet in order to plan effective and progressive learning experiences for children and to discuss the significance of language structures with children, teachers of literacy, we hypothesised, did need to have this knowledge.

With these considerations in mind, we developed the following component list of subject knowledge in literacy. In each component, we included the relevant knowledge of content, of pedagogy and of learners. Our working hypothesis was that effective teachers of literacy were likely to have a sounder grasp of this subject knowledge than less effective teachers, and the list formed the basis of the subject knowledge instrument we developed for the second phase of observation and interview.

1   word- and sub-word-level knowledge (e.g. phonemic, spelling and vocabulary knowledge);
2   sentence-level knowledge (e.g. grammatical knowledge);
3   text-level knowledge (e.g. knowledge of text types and structures);
4   supra-textual knowledge (e.g. knowledge and critical appreciation of a range of texts).

This component list does require some exemplification to make it clearer. The expanded list, with examples, follows.

Word- and sub-word-level knowledge

- Phonological and alphabetical knowledge: e.g. knowing letter shapes, knowing that words are built up from letters and letter groups with sound values, knowing that a crucial unit in word attack is the syllable with its initial onset sound and its rime, knowing that analogy is a useful strategy in word recognition (having read *peak* makes it easier to read *beak*).
- Knowledge of spelling strings and patterns: e.g. knowing the patterned basis to spelling (there are a limited number of possible spellings for individual syllables), understanding the role of morphemes in spelling (*-ed*, *-ing*, *sub-*, *pre-*, etc.). Also knowing about typical sequences of development in children's abilities to spell conventionally.
- Vocabulary knowledge: e.g. being able to help children to explore word origins and extend vocabulary, knowing about synonyms, antonyms, homonyms and homophones. Also understanding the importance of developing a core of words that are instantly recognisable to children.

Sentence-level knowledge

- Grammatical knowledge: e.g. knowing word classes (i.e. nouns, verbs, adjectives), grammatical functions in sentences (i.e. subject, verb, object), syntax (i.e. word order and the relationship between words and in sentences), and having command of suitable language with which to discuss these features with children. Also having an understanding about the ways in which children acquire syntactic knowledge.
- Punctuation knowledge: e.g. knowing the uses and functions of a range of punctuation marks. Also understanding the likely course of children's learning about these.

Text level knowledge

- Knowledge of text structures: e.g. knowing that types of text (stories, arguments, explanations, instructions) are structured differently, understanding the structural differences between types of text and being able to talk meaningfully about these differences with children.
- Knowledge of text features: e.g. knowing that stories have plots, events and characters, understanding typical developmental sequences in children's appreciation of these elements.
- Knowledge of comprehension processes: e.g. understanding the importance of previous knowledge, of question setting and of adopting appropriate strategies for reading. Also understanding how comprehension develops and might be facilitated.
- Knowledge of composition processes: e.g. understanding elements of the writing process such as drafting, revising, editing, proof-reading. Also understanding likely developmental sequences in children's abilities to use these processes.

Supra-textual knowledge

- Knowledge of literature for children: e.g. knowing a range of suitable literature and authors for particular children, having some understanding of quality in children's literature, understanding how to enhance children's responses to literature.
- Knowledge of the purposes and functions of various texts in social discourse: e.g. knowing the ways in which text function and structure are linked.
- Knowledge of the ways in which literacy enables learning in a range of areas and of how opportunities for such development may be created.

Hypotheses regarding teacher development

In addition to the above hypotheses regarding the characteristics of effective teachers of literacy, we also explored the ways in which teachers developed these characteristics. Our initial hypothesis here was that simply attending an in-service course would be insufficient to promote teacher development and that this demanded a much more extensive and elaborated experience of learning, understanding and internalising knowledge about how children become literate and how effective teachers promote this. Wider research into teachers' professional development suggests that a significant factor is the opportunity, with appropriate stimulus and support, to construct, over a period of time, personal, practical theories about teaching in their subject. Our hypothesis was that experiences such as action research or involvement with projects such as the National Writing Project would emerge as significant catalysts in the development of effective teachers of literacy.

The main findings of the research: a summary

At this point in the book, we will give a brief preview of some of the major findings of the research. Broadly speaking, we found that the effective teachers of literacy in this study tended to:

1   Believe that it is important to make it explicit that the purpose of teaching literacy is to enable their pupils to create meaning using text. While almost all teachers would endorse this aim, the effective teachers of literacy that we studied were very specific about how literacy activities at the whole text, word and sentence levels contributed to such meaning creation.

2   Centre much of their teaching of literacy around 'shared' texts; that is, texts that the teacher and children either read or wrote together. Shared texts were used as a means of making the connections between text-, sentence- and word-level knowledge explicit to children, both as a vehicle for teaching specific ideas at text, sentence and word levels and for showing how the features of words, sentences and texts work together.

3   Teach aspects of reading and writing such as decoding and spelling in a systematic and highly structured way and also in a way that made clear to pupils why these aspects were necessary and useful.

4   Emphasise to their pupils the functions of what they were learning in literacy. Thus the rules of grammar, for example, were not usually taught as discrete items of knowledge but as connected features that would help children to improve their writing for specific purposes.

5   Have developed strong and coherent personal philosophies about the teaching of literacy, which guided their selection of teaching materials and approaches. These philosophies enabled them to pull together their knowledge, skills and beliefs in this area and helped to give greater co-ordination to their teaching of literacy.

6   Have well-developed systems for monitoring children's progress and needs in literacy and use this information to plan future teaching.

7   Have extensive knowledge about literacy, although not necessarily in a form that could be abstracted from the context of teaching it.

8   Have had considerable experience of in-service activities in literacy, both as learners and, often, having themselves planned and led such activities for their colleagues.

9   Be, or have been, the English subject co-ordinator in their schools.

We will use this pattern of characteristics as a framework for exploring the implications of our findings for the initial training and continuing professional development of teachers of literacy.

The outline of the book

There are eight chapters in the book:

Chapter 1: *Effective teaching and effective teachers.* In this chapter, we will review previous research that has provided us with insights into the characteristics of effective teachers. We will go on to apply these insights to such research as there is into effective teachers of literacy.

Chapter 2: *Investigating effective teachers of literacy.* Here we give an account of how we conducted the research into effective teachers of literacy.

Chapter 3: *Effective teachers of literacy in action.* Here we present the main features of the literacy-teaching practices that characterised the effective teachers we studied.

Chapter 4: *The subject knowledge of effective teachers of literacy.* In this chapter, we present and discuss our findings concerning the subject knowledge that underpinned the work of the effective teachers of literacy.

Chapter 5: *Teachers' beliefs about literacy teaching.* Here we discuss the beliefs and belief systems about literacy and its teaching that appeared to guide the effective teachers in their practice.

Chapter 6: *Knowledge, beliefs and practice in effective teachers of literacy.* These three sets of characteristic features were working together in the effective teachers of literacy and in this chapter we discuss the ways in which these connections were shown, illustrating this through detailed case studies of two teachers.

Chapter 7: *Becoming an effective teacher of literacy.* One of the main questions guiding the research concerned the professional development experiences that had enabled our main target group of teachers to become effective in the teaching of literacy. In this chapter we discuss our findings about this.

Chapter 8: *Conclusions and implications.* Here we summarise the major findings of the research and draw out what we consider to be its main implications for policy and practice.

1 Effective teaching and effective teachers

In this chapter, we will discuss the principal issues emerging from a review of the literature relevant to our research project. Three main areas are covered:

1 effective teaching and effective teachers;
2 the nature of literacy, i.e. what needs to be taught;
3 the effective teaching of literacy and what effective teachers of literacy might be expected to know and do.

Effective teaching and effective teachers

The literature on effective teaching has a number of dominant themes. These include school effect issues as well as issues related to the likely characteristics of effective teachers. Given the lack of value-added data on which to base valid assertions, variations in children's literacy achievements must be treated cautiously. It has been suggested that a child's background (prior learning, intelligence, home background, parents, etc.) contributes 85 per cent to what is learned in school, only the remaining 15 per cent being contributed by schooling (Harrison, 1996). This seems a pessimistic estimate and is confounded by the evidence that individual children vary hugely in terms of the experiences of literacy they get in school.

It is also the case that particular school effects are unlikely to affect all children equally (Allington, 1984). Stanovich (1986) has identified the 'Matthew effect', whereby school settings enable those pupils who are already rich in literacy experience to get richer, while those who are poor in literacy experience simply get poorer. Such an effect may well explain why, even though schools and teachers can make a difference, the rank order of children entering school may not be greatly altered by school experience (Raban, 1991).

The Effective Teachers of Literacy research project focused on the contribution made by the teacher and the school to what children learn. Research on school effectiveness suggests that variations in children's literacy performance may be related to three types of effect: whole school, teacher and methods/materials. Of these, the consensus is that the effect of the teacher is the most significant (Barr, 1984; Adams 1990). According to Alexander *et al.* (1992), effective teaching depends on the successful application of teachers' 'curricular expertise', by which they mean 'the subject knowledge, the understanding of how children learn and the skills needed to teach subjects successfully'.

Most of the research into effective teaching is generic rather than specific to literacy teaching. A range of types of study has been used to make statements about effective teaching and effective teachers. In the 1970s, a number of large-scale studies in the USA attempted to look at teacher effect by searching for links between teacher classroom behaviour and pupil achievement. Some, but not all, of these studies included reading and word recognition tests in the measures used to calculate output. Brophy and Good (1986) offer a useful review of the area.

More recent studies have taken a more complex view of the classroom and used multifaceted methods of research. Studies such as that of Bennett *et al.* (1984) have looked at the classes of teachers deemed effective and Mortimore *et al.* (1988) studied teaching in junior schools. At the same time official inspections by Her Majesty's Inspectorate (HMI) have sought to identify and describe effective teaching.

While the research offers little literacy-specific information, it does give a range of findings concerning:

- teacher classroom behaviour, such as classroom management, task setting, task content and pedagogic skills – 'the skills needed to teach subjects successfully', in the words of Alexander *et al.* (1992);
- teacher subject knowledge and beliefs, in which we include content knowledge in a subject, an understanding of how children learn in that subject and the belief systems that interact with and enable such knowledge to be put into operation in the classroom.

These studies are complex, and their conclusions are affected by a wide range of factors. While this suggests that complex instructional problems cannot be solved through simple prescriptions, a number of common characteristic features of effective teaching and teachers have emerged.

Teacher classroom behaviour

Provision of the opportunity to learn

Silcock (1993) argues that the chief finding of research into effective teaching is that effective teachers are those who provide pupils with the maximum opportunity to learn. It is certainly true that the importance of the quantity of instruction that children receive is the most consistently replicated finding in effectiveness research (Brophy and Good, 1986). This has been confirmed by research such as that of Stallings *et al.* (1977), who identified thirty-three factors associated with successful pupil reading test scores. Some of these were factors related to organisational issues rather than to teachers: for example, smaller classes showed greater pupil gains. But it was also found that pupils who spent most time being instructed or working on academic tasks and less time in games and socialising made the most progress.

Care must be taken, however, in suggesting that learning can be judged by time allocation. Two caveats arise. First, teachers are likely to be different in the efficiency of their use of similar amounts of time. Leinhardt and Greeno (1986), for example, noted that the efficiency of experienced teachers allowed them to perform complex procedures in a fraction of the time taken by novices. Second, time allocated to learning does not necessarily equate exactly with time spent on learning. Bennett *et al.* (1980) found that children were actually engaged in tasks for only 58 per cent of the time allocated to mathematics in primary classes. Rosenshine (1979) demonstrated that during the average 85-minute lesson time allocated to primary reading, pupils were engaged in the task for an average of only 63 of those minutes. Research has confirmed (e.g. Brophy and Good, 1986) that the features of classroom life most consistently linked with pupils' achievement were those that suggested maximum pupil engagement in academic activities and minimal time spent unengaged, such as during transitions from one activity to another.

Classroom organisation

There is some evidence that pupil achievement also relates to effective classroom organisation. Students who were more likely to achieve were those who could get help when they required it and who knew what options were available to them on completion of their work. The success rate of seatwork (i.e. work set by the teacher and done independently by children while seated) tends to be high, and research suggests that students who move at a brisk pace through small tasks that yield a high success rate are most likely to be successful.

Pressley *et al.* (1996), in investigating the teaching of literacy teachers nominated as effective, found that they used a combination of whole class, group and individual teaching. About half their time was spent in whole class teaching, with the amount of group teaching varying according to the age group taught. Fifty-five of the eighty-three teachers studied used ability groups in their teaching. A similar picture emerges from British research (Alexander, 1992; Bennett and Dunne, 1992) and suggests that effective teachers make decisions about the grouping of children in their classrooms according to the needs both of the children and of the tasks in which they are involved. Classroom organisational patterns are chosen for their fitness for the teacher's purpose at the time.

Task setting (matching)

The level of success that pupils achieve appears to be related to the tasks they are set. Bennett *et al.* (1984) found that in infant classes, number and language tasks were matched to the pupil's abilities in only about 40 per cent of cases. In the first term of junior schooling this fell to around 30 per cent, with three-quarters of the tasks set for high attainers being badly matched to their abilities. In these cases, the children could succeed at the tasks but were unlikely to gain new knowledge or skills. Brophy and Good (1986) stressed that effective teachers demanded productive engagement with the task, prepared well and matched the tasks to the abilities of the children.

The Beginning Teacher Education Study (Powell, 1980) studied experienced teachers and highlighted possible conflicts between the need to maximise children's engagement with tasks and the need to ensure a high success rate. Children seem more likely to be engaged in activities directed by the teacher (Stallings *et al.*, 1978; Brophy and Good, 1986) than during independent seatwork, but teacher-directed activities for a class or group expose all members of the group to the same content and can limit the attainment of the brightest and become too difficult for the slowest. Differentiated seatwork can address the problem but requires more complex preparation and class management, which may result in lower engagement rates and increase the differences between the high and low achievers in the class, despite increased overall success rates (Denham and Lieberman, 1980). This may result in a tension between the match of the task to pupil ability and the level of pupil engagement.

Task content

The nature of the tasks that are set for children may also be related to achievement. Hiebert (1983) reports that lower-ability groups tended to spend more time on decoding tasks, while higher-ability groups were more likely to engage in critical reasoning tasks. In the classes studied by Bennett *et al.* (1984), 75 per cent of language tasks demanded the practising of existing knowledge, concepts or skills rather than revision, the extension of existing knowledge or acquisition of new knowledge. A general pattern of task distribution suggested that pupils were introduced to new concepts and skills near the start of the term but were allowed little chance to consolidate them. Later in the term, knowledge acquisition declined and was replaced by more and more practice. The nature of the tasks planned also suggested that the teachers offered large amounts of revision and practice to the high achievers and a high level of knowledge acquisition to the low attainers, who might very well have needed more practice. This suggests that teachers need to ensure that the type of task, not simply the amount of task content, is matched to the needs of the pupil.

Teaching skills

The skills underpinning effective instruction have been investigated in a number of studies. Westerhof (1992) confirmed the Stallings suggestion that direct teaching involving questioning and teacher feedback correlated positively with pupil achievement, although this was found to be true only in mathematics lessons and not for other subjects. Powell (1980) also found that the largest gains occurred in those classes where teachers maximised instruction time (and minimised preparation) and spent most of their time instructing the children and monitoring their work. Clark *et al.* (1979) report a range of studies that emphasise the importance of teachers structuring the lesson content through clear presentation, feedback to student responses and attempting to improve incorrect or incomplete responses.

In the presentation of tasks to children, vagueness, false starts and discontinuities appear to reduce student achievement (Smith and Land, 1981), and a mixture of questions demanding different levels of thinking produces the best achievement in middle school science (Tobin and Capie, 1982). Questioning is thought to have a role to play in direct teaching. Samson *et al.* (1987) recommend questioning that ensures participation and mastery of academic content, provides adequate wait time and uses higher-order questions. Wragg (1984) emphasises the value of higher-order questioning in which children are involved in thinking or reasoning despite the finding (Galton and Simon, 1980) that most primary school lessons were didactic, with very few open-ended or enquiring questions. Mortimore *et al.* (1988) found that only 2 per cent of questions asked in junior classrooms were challenging. Brophy and Good (1986) make recommendations from their review of research that include the need to ensure that questions are clear, that all children are asked questions, that the pace of questioning is adjusted to the task, and that children are given sufficient wait time to answer. They also stress that it is important for questions to elicit correct answers, although, as new material is learned, the error rate will inevitably rise as a result of children being stretched (Bennett *et al.*, 1984).

The pace of introduction of material must depend on the capabilities of the children in the class. Brophy and Good (1986) report that in classes where children succeeded with relative ease the pace could be brisker, whereas in classes where children started at a lower ability level, slow introduction of material was necessary. Brisk pace has been associated with high achievement in reading by a number of researchers.

More recent characterisations of teaching have stressed the importance of teachers demonstrating, or modelling, the learner behaviour they wished to encourage. Pressley *et al.* (1996), for example, when investigating the teaching of literacy teachers deemed as effective, found that all of them reported overt modelling of reading for students on a daily basis. This included reading aloud to students, the modelling of comprehension strategies, modelling the writing process and demonstrating their own love of writing and reading. A crucial element of the reciprocal teaching strategy developed by Palincsar and Brown (1984) was the active demonstration by teachers of high-level cognitive operations. Reciprocal teaching has been shown to enhance pupil learning significantly in a number of studies (Palincsar and Brown, 1984; Gilroy and Moore, 1988; Moore, 1988).

Teacher–pupil interaction

Teacher–pupil interaction in classes has also been a major focus of interest. Appropriate pace, interaction with children, monitoring of children at work and feedback all appear to be features of effective teaching and play a part in ensuring high levels of task engagement as well as providing feedback to pupils. Brophy and Good (1986) recommend that teachers, in handling children's responses to questions, should train all children to respond, even with a 'don't know', acknowledge correct responses positively but avoid over-praising, affirm correct parts of answers and rephrase incorrect parts, and indicate incorrect answers by simple negation.

The studies reviewed by Brophy and Good also include teacher interaction and the monitoring of classroom activity, and they recommend careful direct teaching followed by guided practice in which teachers monitor the success of children carefully and intervene where necessary. More recently, the metaphor of 'scaffolding' has been used to explain the nature of effective teacher–pupil interaction (Bruner, 1986). Scaffolding suggests that by careful support the teacher can enable children to operate at higher levels of cognitive functioning than they would achieve on their own. Wood (1988) uses evidence from observations of parent–child interactions to exemplify the effectiveness of this approach in terms of learning gains.

In the Texas Teacher Effectiveness study, Brophy and Evertson (1976) reported that certain teacher characteristics were associated with effectiveness, and these affected patterns of pupil–teacher relationships. Effective teachers were likely to be businesslike and task-oriented teachers who interacted with students in a primarily teacher–student relationship and spent most time on academic activities. The effective teachers were also likely to assume personal responsibility for pupil achievement, and reveal, in interviews, feelings of efficacy and control, a tendency to organise their classrooms and plan activities proactively on a daily basis, and a 'can do' attitude to solving problems. These teachers were likely, when faced with a problem, to redouble their efforts rather than give up, particularly those teachers who were successful with lower-achieving children. These characteristics have also been observed in other studies (Brophy and Good, 1986), and a recent report on mathematics teaching practice in a number of countries (OFSTED, 1996) gives a similar picture.

Summary

In the United Kingdom, HMI (DES, 1988), deriving evidence from school inspections, built up a picture of what constitutes effective teaching, nominating several contributing factors, which overlap considerably with those emerging from the research reviewed above:

- classroom organisation
- planning and preparation
- matching of work to pupils
- classroom interaction
- mastery of subject
- competence in teaching skills.

Of this list, the factor that had been least studied, until quite recently, was teachers' mastery of their subjects. This factor will be discussed in the following section.

Teachers' subject knowledge and beliefs

It has been claimed (Ausubel, 1968) that the most important factor determining what learners take from any experience of teaching is what they already know about what is being taught. Such a view is readily accepted by most researchers and theorists in the field of learning and rests on an analysis of learning as the progressive building, reshaping and fine tuning of learners' schemas; that is, their mental maps of various aspects of the world around them (Rumelhart, 1980). If this constructivist view of learning is accepted, then in order to maximise children's learning, teachers need to have ways of taking into account their pre-existing schemas. Bennett (1993) argues that teachers are generally poor at doing this, which he attributes to an often fairly inadequate grasp of the subject being taught. Bennett asks the crucial question: 'How can teachers teach well knowledge that they do not fully understand?' (p.6).

Such a concern for teachers' subject knowledge has underpinned the research of Shulman (1986) in the USA, who argues that research on teaching that has led to the insights described in the previous section of this review has almost always ignored a key feature of classroom life: the subject matter. This subject knowledge has since become a key focus for research and was given emphasis, for example, by Alexander *et al.* (1992), who stated their belief that 'subject knowledge is a critical process at every point in the teaching process: in planning, assessing and diagnosing, task setting, questioning, explaining and giving feedback'. Shulman (1987) has outlined seven knowledge bases underlying teacher understanding:

1   content knowledge: the amount and organisation of knowledge about a subject in the mind of the teacher;
2   general pedagogical knowledge: knowledge of the broad principles and strategies of classroom management, transcending any one subject area;
3   curriculum knowledge: knowledge of the materials and programmes that support and guide the teaching of a subject;
4   pedagogical content knowledge: knowledge of ways of transforming content in order to represent it for others;
5   knowledge of learners and their characteristics: knowledge and expectations of typical and of particular learners;
6   knowledge of educational contexts: knowledge of particular classrooms, schools, communities and cultures within which education occurs;
7   knowledge of educational ends: knowledge of agreed purposes for and values underpinning educational endeavour.

From this conceptualisation, it is apparent that teachers' subject knowledge embodies a good deal more than their knowledge of the content of what they will teach. It clearly also includes what Alexander *et al.* (1992) refer to as 'an understanding of how children learn'.

Subject knowledge and its use in teaching

While Shulman's conceptualisation of teacher subject knowledge is not universally accepted, evidence seems to be accumulating regarding the importance of subject knowledge in effective teaching. Borko *et al.* (1988), for example, found that student teachers with strong subject knowledge tended to plan lessons in less detail and were more responsive to the needs of particular groups of pupils. Grossman *et al.* (1989) found that student teachers with specialist knowledge tended to teach it in a way that encouraged children to develop complex conceptual structures of their own. Students without this knowledge tended simply to 'deliver' the content prescribed, relying more heavily on the abilities of children to memorise it. Bennett's research (Bennett and Turner-Bissett, 1993) into student teacher development found that students with specialist knowledge in music and science were significantly more able to engage their pupils at a conceptual level in these subjects than were students without these specialisms, although the same was not true of students with specialist knowledge in mathematics.

Bennett *et al.* (1993) use Shulman's model of pedagogical reasoning to explain the ways in which expert teachers operate. They see expert teaching as a cycle of intention, comprehension, transformation, instruction, evaluation and reflection. They argue that teachers must comprehend the ideas to be taught, then transform these into pedagogically useful and adaptable forms using a combination of:

- preparation
- representation (choosing ways to represent subject matter to learners)
- instructional selections (choice of teaching approach)
- adaptation (differentiation according to the needs of particular learners).

Each element of this teaching cycle draws upon particular combinations of the teacher's knowledge bases. Transformation, for example, demands a combination of content knowledge, pedagogical content knowledge, curriculum knowledge and knowledge of learners. This model appears to be a useful way of thinking about the ways knowledge, planning, tasks and organisation may be related through the actions of the teacher.

Teachers' beliefs

Alexander *et al.* (1991) define knowledge as 'all that a person knows or believes to be true' (p.371), which suggests that there are some difficulties involved in attempting to disentangle teachers' knowledge from their beliefs. The relationship between teachers' beliefs and teachers' knowledge is complex, but it would clearly be naive to attempt to examine teachers' subject knowledge without taking account of the beliefs and attitudes that are inseparable from it.

In the Effective Teachers of Literacy Project, we explored the ways in which teachers' beliefs interrelated with knowledge and how they worked in operationalising the knowledge of effective teachers in classrooms.

These are clearly not simple issues. Studies of teacher beliefs (e.g. Munby, 1984; Nespor, 1987; Richardson, 1994) suggest that the extent to which teachers adopt new instructional practices in their classrooms relates closely to the degree of alignment between their personal beliefs and the assumptions underlying particular innovatory teaching programmes or methods. Such studies have led to a strong feeling that an understanding of teachers' beliefs is important in understanding teachers' current classroom practices and in designing professional development programmes that seek to change those practices. Harste and Burke (1977) point out, however, that examining implicit beliefs is fraught with problems. If beliefs are implicit they may not be articulated, and as beliefs do not necessarily transfer into practice, they cannot be inferred directly from practice. However, these authors did argue that their research was suggesting that 'despite atheoretical statements, teachers are theoretical in their instructional approach' (p.32). Deford (1985) developed a multiple-choice instrument (the Theoretical Orientation to Reading Profile) that found strong relationships between scores on attitude statements and predictions of classroom behaviour in teaching reading. However, she admits that the extent of the influence of teachers' theoretical orientations is difficult to demonstrate, and replications of her research (e.g. Hoffman and Kugle, 1982) have failed to find such a direct correlation between teachers' theoretical orientations and specific classroom behaviours. Hook and Rosenshine (1979) argue that, by categorising teachers' beliefs into belief systems, clear differences can be found between teachers in terms of their classroom behaviour. This suggests that teachers develop their own relatively coherent theoretical positions regarding teaching. It is the nature and extent of such coherence that the Effective Teachers of Literacy Project sought to investigate and, particularly, whether effective teachers had such coherent theoretical positions underpinning their teaching.

Literacy and its teaching

We are defining literacy as the ability to read and write accurately and effectively in order to accomplish socially important tasks. Such tasks, for children of school age, include learning the basics of reading and writing and developing the ability to use reading and writing to learn in other subjects. This demands particular types of knowledge and a range of skills.

Literacy knowledge

This knowledge has a number of aspects that are essential in order to be a successful reader and writer. These include knowledge of language and its components and knowledge of a variety of socially important texts.

Linguistic and metalinguistic knowledge

There are a number of ways to describe the English language: the model that underpins the National Curriculum for English was developed in the Kingman Report (DES, 1988). The various elements of linguistic knowledge that children need in order to be literate include elements such as letter recognition, sound–symbol correspondence and grammatical conventions. They also include knowledge about how these elements operate in the English language, and the importance of this *metalinguistic* knowledge has been stressed by a number of researchers (e.g. Downing and Valtin, 1984). In order to become fully literate, children need both knowledge *of* language (how to use it) and knowledge *about* language (how it is structured).

This knowledge can be summarised at a number of levels: word and sub-word level (phonics, spelling and vocabulary); sentence level (grammar and punctuation); and text level (features of texts and genres). At each of these levels, a more detailed list of knowledge components can be outlined:

1 Word and sub-word level:
   - phonological and alphabetical knowledge, e.g. letter shape recognition, knowing that words are built up from letters and letter groups

with sound values, the ability to recognise rhyme and analyse spoken language;
- knowledge of spelling strings and patterns, e.g. knowing the patterned basis to spelling (there are a limited number of possible spellings for individual syllables), understanding the role of morphemes in spelling (*-ed, -ing, sub-, pre-,* etc.);
- vocabulary knowledge, e.g. word origins, extended vocabulary, synonyms, antonyms, homonyms and homophones.

2 Sentence level:
- grammatical knowledge, e.g. knowing word classes (i.e. nouns, verbs, adjectives), grammatical functions in sentences (i.e. subject, verb, object), syntax (i.e. word order and the relationship between words in sentences);
- punctuation knowledge, e.g. knowing the uses of a range of punctuation marks and the ways these function as meaning markers in written texts.

3 Text level:
- knowledge of text structures, e.g. knowing that types of text (stories, arguments, explanations, instructions) are structured differently, understanding the structural differences between types of texts;
- knowledge of text features, e.g. knowing about plot, events and characters in stories.

One area of debate about this knowledge has been the degree to which knowledge of linguistic terminology is necessary. Researchers have referred to the 'glass effect' (Kavanagh and Mattingley, 1972) to illustrate the central issue. This image suggests that language can either be considered transparent, like glass, in that it can be used effectively but is rarely discussed in itself and so appears transparent. Alternatively, it can, like glass, be studied and discussed in itself, in which case it is made opaque. In teaching children literacy, both aspects of the image are appropriate. Teachers certainly aim for children to use language effortlessly, that is without needing to think explicitly about how they are using it. However, in order to teach language it is necessary for teachers to discuss it with children, and this requires a shared vocabulary. Thus children of primary school age do need to have some knowledge of linguistic terminology.

Text knowledge

A further area of knowledge for children is their awareness and knowledge of socially important texts. This includes a knowledge of the accepted canon of literature, suitable for their ages, that would allow them to play an appropriate role in an educated society. Children also need to know the conventions of accessing texts in the contemporary world, including book handling and the use of computers and other information sources.

Literacy skills

Knowledge of and about the English language is a necessary but not a sufficient condition to ensure effective literacy. Literacy is more completely defined as the ability to use this knowledge effectively; that is, as a group of linked competences. Moreover, it is necessary for children to be able to vary their use of these competences to fit their immediate context. This flexible use of literacy skills and knowledge separates the effective literacy user from the ineffective.

The skills of literacy necessarily include the ability to use the knowledge specified above at the word, sentence and text levels. Children need, for example, to be able to use phonic, graphic, syntactic and contextual information to read words and sentences. They also need to use their knowledge of words, spelling patterns and grammatical sequences to write coherently. Their skills must also include all levels of comprehension and composition.

Comprehension includes:

- the ability to understand words and other meaningful units of text on a literal level;
- the ability to use a range of strategies to identify the meanings of words;
- the ability to go beyond the text by making inferences based on the text and knowledge of the wider world;
- the ability to interrogate the text for specific items of information;
- the ability to compare and appreciate texts.

Composition of texts depends on a wide range of skills, including:

- letter-formation and handwriting skills;
- spelling skills;
- the ability to create appropriate sentences;
- the identification of an audience, purpose and aim for a piece of writing;
- the use of the conventions of a genre to shape writing effectively;
- the ability to plan, revise, redraft and edit writing.

The use of comprehension and composition skills involves children in a further level of metalinguistic awareness. Literacy users must understand the purposes and functions of literate activities and have a degree of awareness of the skills they use to achieve these. It is also useful for them to be able to monitor and regulate their comprehension strategies and their composing processes. Studies suggest, for example, that successful readers are aware of when they do not understand what they are reading and can then adopt an appropriate strategy to remedy this situation. Similarly, successful writers are those who have a clear understanding of the writing task (including the demands of its audience) and create mental structures that monitor their writing against their intentions. As with knowledge about language, it is useful for children and teachers to have a shared vocabulary about the skills involved in literacy so that they can be discussed as part of teaching and learning.

Finally, to be an effective literacy user, it is not enough to learn the appropriate skills and knowledge without being able to use them flexibly in a range of contexts, both in and out of school. As with all learning, the transfer of literacy skills from the context in which they were learned to contexts in which they are useful is problematic. For this reason, children must use reading and writing for a range of purposes and audiences rather than learn simply to read and write in decontextualised situations such as exercises. The position of literacy in schools is therefore somewhat special, in that the skills and knowledge that children acquire also need to be assessed in other contexts as they are being put to use. Literacy is a crucial part of learning in all other curriculum areas.

The National Curriculum for English (DES, 1995) tries to describe these components of literacy learning as part of a curriculum for English on the basis of what is known about the ways in which literacy is learned.

Literacy learning

The acquisition by young children of the skills of reading has received a great deal of research attention. The acquisition of writing, however, has only recently begun to catch up, with fewer large-scale studies.

In the research three basic theoretical positions have been taken, and each of these has been reflected in particular teaching approaches. These three positions are:

1   the view that early literacy acquisition occurs in 'stages', each of which is constrained by a child's maturation;
2   the view that literacy is acquired in a socially 'natural' way similar to the acquisition of speech;
3   views of literacy teaching that stress the necessity of mastering certain skills or elements of formal knowledge.

The first of these positions on literacy learning, heavily rooted in Piagetian views of child development, suggests that the learning has a definite structure and generally follows a hierarchical, usually linear, progression. Researchers interested in the work of Vygotsky have challenged this position, offering evidence of children who do not appear to learn to read and write in the hierarchical way suggested. A major focus of this second position has been to emphasise the knowledge and skills that children acquire in their home settings and to emphasise the qualities of parent–child interaction that support learning. This has led to the use of the concept of scaffolding (Webster *et al.*, 1996; Wood, 1988) in children's literacy learning and to greater attention being given to the role of the family in literacy development (Taylor, 1983; Basic Skills Agency, 1996).

A third position, increasingly prominent in recent debates, rests upon an examination of the skill acquisition of learners. Research in this area has demonstrated the important role of such cognitive features as phonological awareness, the activation of previous knowledge and comprehension monitoring in literacy acquisition.

Each of these positions on literacy acquisition has implications for the teaching of literacy. Each stresses different aspects of literacy acquisition, so each suggests different priorities for teaching. One key area of debate has concerned the relative roles of what Adams (1990) calls *method* and *purpose* in written text and Downing (1979) refers to as *featural* and *functional* concepts about print. These terms refer to the fact that written text is based upon a system whereby symbols represent the sounds of spoken language (method) and is produced with the purpose of conveying meaning (purpose). Different views about the learning of literacy prioritise different aspects, but all suggest that both the method and purpose of written text must be learned.

It would be inappropriate to suggest that the teaching methods implied by each position are necessarily in direct opposition. In very broad terms, a synthesis gleaned from research into how children learn literacy suggests that, while there are broad developmental sequences, these are not the same for each child and may depend heavily on individual circumstances. Similarly, the need for children to acquire specific literacy skills such as the use of phonic knowledge and the ability to spell accurately is important, and research from all groups would suggest this is best done in a meaningful context. Goswami and Bryant (1990) have argued that it is unhelpful to think of literacy development as a series of steps along a linear path. Instead, attention should focus on the wide range of overlapping interdependent processes that make up literacy. These positions are represented in the National Curriculum, which sets out the necessary knowledge and skills and a broad developmental framework while offering considerable scope for a range of methods and practices of interpretation and delivery. It is in the light of these content requirements that the issue of effective teaching, that is, the delivery of the literacy curriculum, becomes a crucial issue for investigation. What is the nature of effective teaching in literacy?

Effective teaching and effective teachers of literacy

There have been numerous attempts to establish the nature of effective teaching in literacy. Most of these have begun by analysing the processes involved in being literate and then argued from this analysis to put forward a model to guide instruction in literacy (e.g. Chall, 1967; Flesch, 1955; Goodman and Goodman, 1979). The argument has been that effective teaching in literacy is that which produces effective literate behaviour in learners. This sounds like an eminently sensible position, but its main problem has been the difficulty that researchers and teachers have found in agreeing on what exactly should count as effective literate behaviour, especially in reading. The major disagreement has centred on the relative importance given in views of literacy to technical skills such as word recognition, decoding and spelling or to higher-order skills such as making meaning. Such lack of agreement has led to proponents of radically different approaches to teaching literacy claiming superiority for their suggested programmes, but using very different criteria against which to judge the success of these programmes.

A good example of the difficulty caused by the use of such different criteria can be seen in the so-called 'first-grade studies' carried out in the USA during the 1960s (Adams, 1990; Barr, 1984). These studies were designed to test the effectiveness of different approaches to the teaching of beginning reading, and a particular strength was that each of the various approaches was tested in several different experiments and, typically, by different research teams. Most commentators now agree that there was no clear overall winner in the first-grade studies (Barr, 1984) or in extensions of the experiments to grade 2 (Dykstra, 1968). An interesting divergence did emerge, however. It appeared that children's reading of words (fluency and decoding) was improved by teaching programmes that specifically targeted decoding skills and knowledge of letter–sound consistencies in words. Their vocabulary knowledge and comprehension, however, were not improved to the same degree. In programmes centred on meaning, the reverse picture tended to be found: children's decoding and phonic knowledge were not improved, whereas they tended to get better at comprehension and developed more positive attitudes towards reading. Given the ambiguity of these results, the great debate about beginning reading instruction raged on (Chall, 1967).

Since the 1960s, however, there has been a very significant shift in the nature of the debate about literacy teaching. Less attention began to be given to the content of what was taught in literacy and rather more to the nature of the contexts in which literacy might best be taught. An approach known in the USA and other parts of the world as 'whole language' (this term is not widely used in the UK, although the teaching approach it denotes does have adherents) emphasises language processes and the creation of learning environments in which children experience authentic reading and writing (Weaver, 1990). Both linguistic and cognitive development are presumed to be stimulated by the experience of reading good literature and of writing original compositions. Whole language theorists and teachers stress that skills instruction should occur within the context of natural reading and writing rather than as decontextualised exercises. The development of literacy tends to be seen as a natural by-product of immersion in high-quality literacy environments.

In contrast, other researchers and teachers argue that learning the code is a critical part of early reading and that children are most likely to become skilled in this when they are provided with systematic teaching in decoding (e.g. Chall, 1967). There is growing evidence that such teaching increases reading ability (Adams, 1990), especially for children who experience difficulties in learning to read (Mather, 1992; Pressley and Rankin, 1994).

Increasingly, the explicit teaching of reading skills is thought of in cognitive science terms, largely because much recent evidence supporting it has been generated by cognitive psychologists. For example, some cognitive scientists believe that the development of strong and complex connections between words and their components (Adams, 1990; Foorman, 1994) follows from explicit instruction in phonemic awareness, letter recognition, attention to the sounds of words, blending of sounds, and practice in reading and writing words to the point that they are automatically recognised and produced. Going beyond word-level decoding, many cognitive scientists conceive of comprehension as the application of particular information processes to text (e.g. relating new text to prior knowledge, asking questions in reaction to text, summarising). Skill in comprehension requires the self-regulated use of such information processes, and such comprehension strategies can be directly taught to children: for example, the activation of prior knowledge before reading, asking oneself questions while reading, and transforming the content of what is read into other forms (see Pressley *et al.* (1992) for an account of psychologically based research into the effects of directly teaching such strategies, and Wray and Lewis (1997) for an account of a curriculum development project based around such ideas).

Naturally, this shift in the terms of the debate has led to a switch in the research agenda, and there have been several studies comparing the effectiveness of teaching programmes using a whole language approach, programmes emphasising traditional decoding, and teaching based on the cognitive science model described above. The evidence is growing that teaching based on whole language principles (i.e. the use of whole texts, good literature and fully contextualised instruction) does stimulate children to engage in a greater range of literate activities, develop more positive attitudes towards reading and writing, and increase their understanding about the nature and purposes of reading and writing (e.g. Morrow, 1990, 1991, 1992; Neuman and Roskos, 1990, 1992). Having said that, however, evidence also indicates that, compared with teaching in which decoding skills are emphasised, whole language teaching programmes have less of an effect upon early reading achievement as measured by standardised tests of decoding, vocabulary, comprehension and writing (Graham and Harris, 1994; Stahl *et al.*, 1994; Stahl and Miller, 1989). Teaching that explicitly focuses on phonemic awareness and letter–sound correspondences does, on the other hand, result in improved performance on such standardised tests (Adams, 1990). Also, teaching that explicitly introduces readers to a range of comprehension strategies develops improved understanding of text

(Palincsar and Brown, 1984). The picture emerging from research is therefore not a simple one.

There is, however, a further issue to explore that has potential bearing on an understanding of the nature of effective literacy teaching and that may, in fact, be the focal point around which apparently conflicting research findings may be synthesised. This concerns the near impossibility of finding, and thus testing, 'pure' teaching approaches in literacy. Close examination of many recent studies that appear to support the explicit teaching of decoding and comprehension strategies suggests that embedded in these programmes there are often many elements of what could be described as whole language teaching, including, for example, the reading of high quality children's literature and daily original writing by children (Pressley *et al.*, 1991, 1992). Similarly, when the programmes described by whole language advocates are examined closely, it is quite apparent that they do contain a good deal of systematic teaching of letter–sound correspondences, for example (*cf.* Holdaway, 1979). These teaching approaches, in fact, are tending to become more and more alike, and commentators such as Adams (1991) have suggested that there is no need for a division between teaching approaches styled as 'whole language' or 'explicit code teaching' in orientation. What has emerged in recent years is a realisation that explicit decoding and comprehension instruction are most effectively carried out in the context of other components. As Adams puts it in her comprehensive review of research into beginning reading:

> In both fluent reading and its acquisition, the reader's knowledge must be aroused interactively and in parallel. Neither understanding nor learning can proceed hierarchically from the bottom up. Phonological awareness, letter recognition facility, familiarity with spelling patterns, spelling–sound relationships, and individual words must be developed in concert with real reading and real writing and with deliberate reflection on the forms, functions, and meanings of texts.
>
> (1990: p.422)

Such rapprochement between previously contrasting positions brings to the fore a new hypothesis which suggests that effective literacy teaching is multifaceted (e.g. Adams, 1990; Cazden, 1992; Duffy, 1991; Stahl *et al.*, 1994). That is to say that effective teaching often integrates letter- and word-level teaching with explicit instruction of comprehension processes and sets these within a context meaningful to the children in which they read and write high-quality whole texts. Such an approach implies an informed selection by the teacher from a range of teaching techniques and approaches on the basis of a detailed understanding of the multifaceted nature of literacy and of the needs of a particular group of children. It does not, as Rose (1996) points out, mean the naive use of a range of teaching methods in the hope that, like shotgun pellets, at least some of them will hit the target.

The evidence so far available, therefore, about the effective teaching of literacy supports what might be called a 'reasoned eclecticism' in the approaches teachers adopt. The focus of our research was to consider what it was that effective teachers knew and believed about this teaching, and how this contributed to their effectiveness.

2 Investigating effective teachers of literacy

An overview of the project

The aim of the Effective Teachers of Literacy Project was to examine the practices, beliefs and knowledge of a group of teachers identified as effective at teaching literacy and to check these against the practices, beliefs and knowledge of a group of teachers not so identified – a validation group.

To do this, we identified two main sample groups:

1   the main sample of 228 primary teachers identified as effective in the teaching of literacy;
2   the validation sample of seventy-one primary teachers not so identified.

All these teachers completed a questionnaire designed to enquire into their beliefs about literacy and literacy teaching approaches, their feelings about children's needs in literacy development, their reported use of a range of teaching techniques, and their professional development experience in literacy.

We then identified sub-samples of the two main samples, including:

1   a sub-sample of twenty-six teachers taken from the main group of teachers identified as effective in the teaching of literacy;
2   a validation sub-sample of ten of the primary teachers not so identified taken from the validation group.

The teachers in both these sub-samples were twice observed teaching and then interviewed about each of these teaching episodes. The first observation/interview focused on teaching strategies, classroom organisation and the genesis of these in terms of these teachers' experiences of professional development. The focus in the second interview was on lesson content and teachers' subject knowledge. During the second interview, teachers completed a 'quiz' designed to test their knowledge about aspects of literacy.

An interview was also carried out with the eighteen headteachers of the teachers in both sub-samples. We also, except in the case of reception classes, collected two sets of reading test results of the children being taught by these teachers. One of these sets indicated the children's reading abilities before they arrived in this teacher's class and the other these abilities after a year in this class. These two sets of results were used to provide an objective measure of the effectiveness of these teachers in teaching literacy.

In the rest of this chapter, we give a detailed account of the procedures we used in the project to identify and select participating teachers, and to gather evidence from them about their practices, beliefs and knowledge.

Identifying effective teachers of literacy

Careful identification of effective teachers of literacy was at the heart of the project but was by no means simple. First, there are areas of disagreement about what constitutes effectiveness. This can be judged in a number of ways:

- the effectiveness of the teachers judged by professional colleagues;
- the effectiveness of the teachers judged by outside bodies;
- the outcomes of teaching in terms of pupil progress.

We defined an effective teacher as one whose class made more than the expected amount of progress at literacy learning during the academic year, whose headteacher confirmed that the test results of the class taught by the teacher demonstrated more than the expected gains in reading performance in the previous academic year, and whose school, or class, was nominated as effective at teaching literacy by local education authority (LEA) advisory staff.

The project involved effective teachers of literacy throughout England. Teachers in thirteen LEAs were included in the study so that they represented a range of geographical locations, catchment areas and types of authority (county, metropolitan area, city). In each of these LEAs, the directors of education/chief education officers and senior advisers/inspectors with responsibility for English and/or primary education were invited to identify around thirty primary teachers whom they considered to have demonstrated their effectiveness in teaching literacy. The teachers identified worked in a representative range of schools in that particular authority in terms of school type and social distribution.

In all cases where it was possible (some of the nominated teachers were headteachers themselves), the headteachers of the nominated teachers were contacted by telephone. They were asked to ascertain whether, first, they agreed that the teachers concerned could be classed as effective teachers of literacy and, second, whether this could be supported by objective data about the literacy gains of the pupils in his/her class. No headteacher declined to agree with the advisers' judgements about the effectiveness of their teachers. However, there were a number who could not support this judgement with objective pupil achievement data. Where this was so, these teachers were dropped from the sample.

Where available, the OFSTED (Office for Standards in Education) reports for the schools in which these teachers taught were also consulted. Although obviously not identifying them by name, these reports provided no evidence that the teaching of literacy of any of the teachers in our sample was anything less than satisfactory or better.

Staff of the PIPS (Performance Indicators in Primary Schools) project, based at the University of Durham, were contracted to supply the names of a number of effective teachers of literacy. These names were selected by interrogating their database of test scores, including reading tests and ability scales, so that the results could have a 'value-added' component. All the heads of schools in which these teachers were located were contacted and permission sought by the PIPS project to share the names with us. This source of data was particularly useful in that it allowed us to include some reception teachers in our sample. It is generally not possible to obtain standardised reading test results at the beginning and end of the reception year. The value-added PIPS data, however, allowed us to locate a number of reception teachers whose classes had made more than the expected gains in reading during their first year.

Twelve grant maintained primary schools and fifty-five independent mixed schools covering the 3–5, 5–11 or 7–11 age ranges were identified on the basis that they were located in the same geographical areas as the initial teacher sample, and the headteachers of each of these schools were contacted. The same procedures were followed to verify the effectiveness of the teachers from this sector, and seven questionnaires were sent to teachers in grant maintained schools and twenty to teachers in independent schools.

By the above means, we selected 368 teachers to whom we mailed the initial questionnaire. Completed questionnaires were returned by 228 of these and analysed a completion rate of almost 62 per cent.

Selecting the validation teachers

In selecting a validation sample of teachers we aimed to include teachers who were likely to represent the full normal range of effectiveness in teaching literacy. Our strategy was to focus upon teachers who we knew would be unlikely to be designated in their schools as particular experts in the teaching of literacy because they had been given curricular responsibility for a completely different area. The validation sample, therefore, consisted of mathematics co-ordinators in primary schools, who, we believed, were likely to represent the full range of expertise in teaching literacy in schools.

The sample was selected by the use of the *Primary Education Directory* and the targeting of schools in the LEAs in which the main sample of effective teachers were located. In each LEA, schools were selected at random to represent a range covering where possible:

- small, medium-sized and large schools;
- infant, junior, all-through primary, first and middle schools;
- inner-city, suburban and rural schools.

Questionnaires were sent addressed to 'The Mathematics Co-ordinator' in these schools and also to the mathematics co-ordinators of eight grant maintained primary schools and fifteen independent schools. A total of 135 questionnaires were sent out and seventy-one valid responses returned – a completion rate of almost 53 per cent.

Choosing teachers to visit

In each questionnaire, respondents were asked if they would be willing to participate further in the research, and a large number of them agreed. From this number a tentative core sample of thirty-two teachers was derived using a sampling frame that aimed to balance the following teacher characteristics:

1   **Age and experience.** A large majority of the effective teachers of literacy were experienced teachers. In the core sample, we over-represented the less experienced teachers in order to gain a better picture of the short- to medium-term effects of initial training. Three teachers with less than five years of teaching experience were visited as part of the effective teachers of literacy sub-sample and one as part of the validation sub-sample.
2   **Gender.** The overwhelming majority of the effective teachers of literacy were female (95.5 per cent), and we over-represented the number of male teachers in the core sample by including two male effective teachers of literacy.
3   **School catchment area.** We tried to achieve a balance between teachers teaching in city, town and country schools.
4   **School type.** We aimed to include teachers working in infant schools and junior schools as well as the all-through primary schools in which the majority of pupils are taught.
5   **Area of the country taught in.** The core sample was spread across the country, including:
    - the North (Tyneside and Durham);
    - the South (Hampshire and Croydon);
    - the South-west (Devon, Dorset and Cornwall);

- the West Midlands (Coventry and Solihull);
- London (Lewisham and Hackney).

6 **Age range taught**. We aimed to achieve a balance between Key Stage 1 and 2 teachers but, because we wanted especially to know about the early teaching of literacy, slightly over-represented the number of reception class teachers.

The headteachers of all the teachers in this tentative core sample were contacted by telephone, and each was asked the following questions.

- Whether he/she had reading test scores for the children taught by the sample teacher which would demonstrate that they had made appropriate progress during their time with that teacher (unless the teacher taught a reception class, in which case test data would not be available).
- Whether such reading test scores would be available for us to copy and take away (given an assurance regarding their confidentiality).
- Whether, in the absence of existing tests showing the gains in literacy made by the children in the class, we would be allowed to administer our own tests of the class.
- Whether he/she would be willing to allow us to observe the teaching of the sample teacher and then interview the teacher (sample teachers were also asked if they were willing for this to happen).
- Whether he/she would be willing to be interviewed about the work of the sample teacher.

If the answers to each of these questions were acceptable, that teacher was confirmed as a member of the core sample and an appointment made for the first observation and interview. Where this was not the case, that teacher was dropped from the core sample and an alternative candidate with similar characteristics was approached.

By such means we selected thirty-one teachers whom we planned to observe and interview. However, for reasons beyond our control, it proved impossible for us to find mutually convenient times to observe/interview all of these teachers. In the event, twenty-six effective teachers of literacy were visited on two occasions, observed and interviewed.

The same process was followed for teachers in the validation sample. They were, generally, less keen to be interviewed and less likely to offer us access to their test results. However, thirteen teachers were selected, and ten of these were visited on two occasions.

Test data about children's progress

Two sets of results of standardised test data for the classes taught by these teachers were collected and examined. We needed to obtain test results derived from testing of the children on two occasions with an interval of about one year. In some schools this was a regular practice, and the results of school tests for either the previous June or March (schools varied in their time of administering these tests) and the equivalent months in the current year were collected. In a number of schools test results were available for the previous year but no test was planned for the current year. In these cases, members of the research team administered a test at the appropriate time.

The teachers involved in the study used a range of standardised published tests, each of proven reliability and validity, and generally the data we obtained derived from the administration of the same test two years running. Where a member of the research team administered the test necessary to obtain a second set of results, the same test, or a directly comparable age-appropriate test, was used. This process allowed us to use standardised test results to see whether the children in the class had made the progress at reading that would have been expected during the year they were taught by our teachers. It also caused very little disruption to the normal classroom experience of the teachers and children involved and was, on that count, preferable, we felt, to our administration of a common test to all classes involved in the project.

In the classes of effective teachers of literacy, we found that a majority of children had either maintained or improved their standardised scores in reading, indicating that they had made appropriate progress in comparison with the standardisation sample for the particular test. Average improvements for these classes ranged from 5 to 11 points in standardised scores.

In the classes of the validation sample the picture was much more mixed. Two of the teachers in the validation sample had classes that had made more than the expected level of progress, judged by the results of the standardised tests. Three of the classes had made approximately the progress in reading expected in the year, although the difference and range of scores between pupils was very wide. The other five classes had not made the expected progress through the year, and some pupils' standardised reading scores had decreased. This range was to be expected in a sample that was selected to represent teachers of a range of effectiveness.

It was tempting, but ultimately impossible, to try to compare these teachers and describe some as more effective than others. The tests used by the various schools were different and the results therefore not comparable across schools. Moreover, we knew that the teacher was probably not the only factor in these children's reading success, or lack of it. All our methods aimed to do was simply to identify teachers for whom test results demonstrated that the classes they had taught had made more than the expected level of reading achievement on standardised tests. They also identified teachers whose classes had made less progress at reading.

Headteachers' comments about teachers' effectiveness

The eighteen headteachers of the effective teachers of literacy in our core sample not only confirmed the effectiveness of their teachers by allowing us access to test results. They also confirmed when interviewed that they regarded these teachers as effective. The evidence they gave us included not only test data but also Standard Assessment Task (SAT) results, OFSTED inspection reports, school-based tests and the quality of pupil work. Several also advanced the following additional criteria as evidence of a teacher's effectiveness at teaching literacy:

- Eleven headteachers discussed the personal qualities of the teacher: enthusiasm, character, commitment, knowledge about literacy, enthusiasm and motivation, often with supporting evidence such as attendance at in-service courses, use of classroom display and the ability to enthuse other staff.
- Seven heads cited particular qualities of the teacher's teaching (presumably observed by the head): classroom display, relationship with the children, clear aims, use of paired reading, parental involvement schemes, organisation and planning.
- Six heads saw the teacher's achievements as evidence of effectiveness in teaching literacy: involvement in reading projects, policy writing, schemes of work produced, parental involvement schemes, in-service training offered in school.
- Three of the heads cited external measures: LEA inspection, OFSTED, recommendation of LEA adviser.

Nine headteachers of the validation sample were interviewed and asked whether they considered the teachers to be effective at teaching literacy. Four of the headteachers identified these teachers as effective to some degree, with two expressing confidence that the teacher was a very effective teacher of literacy. Two headteachers suggested that the teachers we had selected were likely to be of only adequate effectiveness in teaching literacy, and two expressed concern about their teachers' performance in teaching literacy. One head declined to respond to this question. The heads based their evaluations on test results in six cases and the personal qualities of the teachers in four. It would, of course, have been unethical of us to inform these heads that their teachers were in our sample to represent teachers who might be lacking in effectiveness in literacy teaching.

Questionnaire design

The questionnaire included the following sections:

- **Background information**. Teacher characteristics such as gender, age, years of experience, subject background, qualifications and phase experience.
- **Professional development experience**. The amount, nature and focus of in-service education and other professional development experienced by the teacher.
- **Beliefs about the teaching of literacy**. The teacher's feelings about particular teaching approaches and their reactions to a range of attitude statements concerning the teaching of literacy.
- **What children need to know in literacy**. The teacher's views on what children at the beginning of Key Stage 1 and 2 need to learn about reading and writing.
- **Teaching strategies**. The reading and writing activities that teachers had used during the immediate past school week.
- **Assessment of children**. The assessment strategies that teachers use and their feelings about the relative importance of several purposes for assessment in literacy.

The quantitative data collected was coded for analysis, mostly in the form of nominal codes, with a very few ordinal codes for dates and Likert-scale data.

The qualitative data collected by the questionnaire included:

- parts of Section 2, professional development;
- Section 4, what children need to know about reading and writing;
- parts of Section 5, teaching strategies used;
- part of Section 6, assessment strategies used.

These sections had asked open questions, which the teachers replied to in writing. Codes for the responses were generated from the data, rather than pre-assigned, so that they would accurately represent the content of responses and the way they were expressed. A copy of the questionnaire is given in Appendix B.

The first observation

The teachers were observed to provide evidence concerning the way their beliefs about teaching, as expressed in the questionnaire, translated into classroom action. The following aspects of the lesson to be observed were listed, and suggestions about the kinds of evidence to be noted were given alongside each.

- the nature of the task(s) set and their context;
- the teacher's differentiation of literacy activities for children with differing needs;

- the motivation and enthusiasm that the teacher was able to generate in the children and the level of the children's engagement with the task set;
- the teacher's monitoring/assessment of the children's progress in literacy in the lesson;
- the environment for literacy provided in the classroom, including the kind of texts used or produced in the lesson;
- the ways in which the teacher demonstrated or modelled literate behaviour;
- the kinds of response the teacher made to the children's reading/writing;
- the kinds of question the teacher asked the children;
- the ways in which the teacher drew the children's attention to the codes of literacy;
- the ways in which the teacher encouraged independence in the children's use of literacy;
- the use of other adults working in the classroom to support literacy work and evidence of home–school links.

Observers focused upon these aspects as they observed a particular lesson and wrote detailed field notes. Following each observation session, observers summarised their field notes under the above headings.

The first interview

To collect the teachers' accounts of the rationale underpinning their selection of classroom organisation and teaching strategies, the first interview schedule focused upon the lesson just observed and included the following sections:

- significant features of the session;
- organisation of the session;
- teaching strategies employed;
- monitoring and assessment of children's learning;
- professional development experience.

A recurrent theme in the interview was the request to teachers to identify how they had learned to do what they had been observed doing in the lesson. The full interview schedule, along with examples of the kinds of prompt questions used, is given in Appendix C.

The second observation

The effective teachers of literacy and the validation teachers were observed a second time with particular attention given to the literacy content of the session and the ways in which this content was represented. The observers focused on the following issues:

- the literacy content of the session;
- any differentiation of the literacy content;
- how the content was represented and any use of linguistic terminology;
- the children's response to the content of the session;
- any follow-up activities signalled to the children.

Field notes and observation reports using these headings were written by observers.

The second interview

The second interview aimed to probe the teacher's perceptions and choice of content by covering the following issues:

- the content of the session;
- why that content had been chosen and taught during the session;
- preparation for the session;
- differentiation of content.

The interview schedule used, together with prompt questions, can be seen in Appendix C.

The headteacher interview schedule

The headteachers were interviewed to explore further their opinions of their teachers' effectiveness as teachers of literacy. The headteacher interview schedule included the following sections:

- the head's estimate of the teacher's effectiveness in teaching literacy and any evidence there was for this judgement;
- any examples that heads could cite of the teacher's effectiveness in teaching literacy;
- what heads considered to have been important experiences for the teacher *en route* to his/her becoming an effective teacher of literacy;
- any professional development measures taken to promote the teacher's effectiveness in teaching literacy;
- any in-school monitoring of the teacher's literacy teaching.

Eighteen headteachers of effective teachers of literacy and nine headteachers of validation teachers were interviewed.

The literacy quiz

In order to provide a measure of teachers' subject knowledge in literacy, they were asked during the second interview session to complete a test.

This we referred to as a 'quiz', and it covered the following items of knowledge.

Grammatical knowledge

The first part of the quiz asked teachers to underline in a sentence words belonging to various word classes: nouns, verbs, adjectives, adverbs, pronouns, conjunctions, prepositions and articles. In this way, we hoped to be able to see which teachers knew these language terms and could recognise them. These basic parts of a sentence were, we felt, the most likely aspects of grammar to be taught to primary-age children, so knowledge of them was likely to be important to the teachers. Our test, of course, was very brief and tested teachers' ability to recognise an example of each word class in a sentence.

Word-level knowledge

The quiz also included a word-segmentation test, which asked teachers to segment words into syllables, phonemes, onset and rime, morphemes, sounds, and units of meaning. These parts of words are important in the teaching of phonological awareness, phonics and some aspects of spelling so, while it was not possible to test teachers' awareness of all sub-word units, these were chosen as representative. This part of the test allowed us to see whether the teachers knew certain technical terms for parts of a word. We also added extra items so that we could see whether teachers were more likely to be able to segment words into sounds and meaning units, terms they were likely to be familiar with, than phonemes and morphemes, terms that they might not know.

Grammatical definitions

A further part of the quiz asked the teachers to comment on a very partial, but traditionally used, definition of a verb, to see whether this was understood to be partial and whether teachers could expand it. This item was chosen to indicate the teachers' levels of understanding about one of the word classes they had been asked to recognise in item 1.

Understanding of language variation

The quiz contained two items about language variation to enable us to gain some insight into teachers' understandings about the nature and structure of standard English. We considered this important, as all teachers are required to teach primary children to use and study standard English, and the ability to do so may be related to their knowledge and ability to recognise it. The first part of the item asked teachers to define accent and dialect, the second to pick out the ways in which a transcribed piece of dialect speech differed from standard English.

Knowledge of children's literature

In addition to knowledge about language, we hypothesised that knowledge of children's literature would be an important part of a teacher's content knowledge. To measure teachers' familiarity with literature, including not only the recommended canon of literature but also the sort of books commonly read by children, the Children's Author Recognition Test (CART–UK), validated by Stainthorp (1996), was used. This simple test asks teachers to distinguish the names of genuine children's authors from foils in a list and offers a measure of teachers' familiarity with children's literature.

Assessment of children's writing and reading

In order to evaluate teachers' knowledge about the way that text-, sentence- and word-level knowledge about literacy might be related, the teachers were asked to compare examples of children's writing and reading.

They were first shown two pieces of children's written work. They were asked to identify as many differences or features of the writing as they could, compare any mistakes and comment on the effectiveness of the two pieces. The pieces used were the instructions for growing cress seeds written by children, and the teachers were all told the background to the task. The pieces were typed, to avoid difficulties with handwriting, but nothing else was corrected. Teachers' responses were taped and subsequently analysed.

They were then asked to look at two examples of children's reading. The aim was to evaluate teachers' knowledge of children's cue use and comprehension strategies, as well as of important features of texts for reading. Two transcriptions of children's attempts to read and retell a version of 'The Emperor's New Clothes' were used. These were shown to the teachers, and they were asked to compare the readings, the mistakes and the retellings. Their accounts were analysed by generating a list of the criteria used by the teachers.

It is important to point out that we were very aware that the 'quiz' we designed would in no way provide a comprehensive measure of the teachers' subject knowledge in literacy. We were, of course, tightly constrained by the amount of time we would have available to administer this quiz and the willingness of the teachers concerned to undertake it. In each area, the items were intended to act as a proxy for substantial bodies of knowledge. A copy of the full quiz is given in Appendix D.

3 Effective teachers of literacy in action

Introduction

The main aim of the project was to explore the factors underpinning the teaching practices of effective teachers of literacy, and in subsequent chapters we will discuss the features of knowledge and beliefs that characterised the effective teachers we studied. First, though, we will outline our findings concerning the literacy-teaching practices that these effective teachers said they used and those that we actually observed them using. In doing this we will show how their knowledge and beliefs were operationalised into classroom practice. It should be remembered that most of the teachers we will describe in this chapter were individuals who could demonstrate high learning gains in literacy for children in their classes.

Different sources of evidence were used to draw conclusions about aspects of teaching practice:

- The questionnaire was used to obtain information about the literacy-teaching activities that teachers reported having used during a normal school week.
- This teacher self-report was checked against our observations of classroom practice.
- The subsequent interviews allowed teachers to describe their practices and offer reasons for their use.

The range of reading activities used

A section of the questionnaire completed by both effective and validation teachers aimed to generate a snapshot of the types of reading and writing activities used in a normal teaching week. A number of reading and writing activities were listed, and teachers were asked to indicate which they had used during the previous week. They were also asked to name up to four other reading or writing activities they had used that week.

The percentage of respondents who used the reading activities listed is summarised in Table 3.1. The results showed that use of reading activities

Table 3.1 Reading activities reported as being used by teachers

Teaching activity	Effective KS1 teachers reporting use of this (%)	Validation KS1 teachers reporting use of this (%)	Effective KS2 teachers reporting use of this (%)	Validation KS2 teachers reporting use of this (%)
Teaching letter sounds/names	92.1	100	43.0	47.8
Used cloze activities	39.2	32.3	55.0	52.2
Used flashcards to teach particular words	40.8	51.6	11.0	19.6
Used sequencing activities	72.8	74.2	52.0	54.3
Read to the class	97.6	96.8	97.0	97.8
Used comprehension activities	36.8	41.9	53.0	71.7
Used a big book with a group of children	73.6	41.9	19.0	21.7
Involved other adults in reading with children	92.8	90.3	80.0	65.2
Heard children read/read with children	98.4	100	97.0	100
Used reading scheme books	87.2	83.9	62.0	69.6
Used phonic exercises	60.0	77.4	45.0	52.2

was, perhaps not surprisingly, related to age phase. While almost all the teachers read to their classes and heard children read, a greater proportion of teachers of Key Stage 1 classes reported that they had:

- taught letter sounds and names
- used flashcards
- used sequencing activities
- used big books
- involved other adults in the teaching of reading
- used reading scheme books
- used phonic exercises.

In the subsequent observations, Key Stage 1 teachers were observed doing all these activities with classes or groups of children, whereas none of these activities were observed in the Key Stage 2 classes. This suggests a clear age-phase differentiation in the choice of teaching activity.

More teachers of Key Stage 2 children reported that they had used cloze activities and comprehension exercises, although in the observations both Key Stage 1 and 2 teachers were observed using these techniques.

There were some differences between the use of reading activities reported by the effective teachers and by teachers in the validation sample. A greater proportion of effective Key Stage 1 teachers reported using big books than did the validation Key Stage 1 teachers. There were also some complex interrelationships between patterns that became clearer when teachers' self-reports and their actual practice were compared. For example, more teachers in the validation sample (at both age phases) reported using phonics exercises and flashcards than did the effective teachers, although both groups were roughly similar in their reported use of teaching letter sounds.

Observation of lessons revealed a different pattern. The lessons we observed of the effective teachers were more likely than those of the validation teachers to include the teaching of letter sounds. There were, however, differences in the ways the two groups approached this. The effective teachers were more likely to spend time looking at letter sounds in the context of reading a big book or a text written by the teacher. They were also more likely to use quick-paced sounds activities, in which they modelled the ways that letters and sounds could be used to help reading. The validation teachers were more likely to offer paper-based exercises using sounds and letters. This difference may underlie the distinction between the two groups implied by the questionnaire finding concerning the use of big books. The effective teachers claimed a greater use of big books, and it seems likely that, although these teachers had chosen this global description of what they were doing, they were in fact engaged in a more complex activity, involving work at both text level and word level. The phonics worksheets apparently preferred by the validation teachers were, on the other hand, not likely to have any other content focus.

We found in general that the effective teachers tended to use activities that involved work at more than one of text, sentence and word levels. They were thus, it seemed, actively assisting their pupils to make connections between these levels. The validation teachers, on the other hand, were more likely to use activities involving work at only one of these levels, limiting the explicit connections their pupils were encouraged to make.

The teachers were also asked in the questionnaire to name any other reading activities they had used during the past week. A vast range of such activities were volunteered and, to enable analysis, these were grouped into categories. For example, 'reading with another child', 'two children reading a book together', 'paired reading' and 'reading with an older child' were all subsumed into the category 'Paired reading'. Forty-two such categories were generated for reading activities, which suggests a very wide range of teaching practices. Of these activities, the most frequently mentioned are

Table 3.2 Other reading activities reportedly used

Reading teaching activity	Effective teachers mentioning this (%)	Validation teachers mentioning this (%)
Paired reading	27.5	29.8
Group reading	26.0	21.1
Children reading aloud	21.6	22.8
Everyone Reading in Class (ERIC)/ silent reading	15.2	7.0
Listening to taped books	14.7	17.5
Reading non-fiction	14.7	14.0
Word building	9.8	15.8
Reading games	8.8	0.0
Computer books	8.8	8.8
Reading environmental print	4.9	1.8
Reading in role play	4.4	0.0
Discussion of authors	7.8	7.0
Phonics/sounds work	6.9	5.3
Reading poems to class	6.9	3.5
Browsing	5.9	0.0
Alphabet activities	4.9	1.8
Dictionary skills activities	4.4	1.8

summarised in Table 3.2, along with the percentage of each sample mentioning them.

Although a high proportion of both groups of teachers claimed to have used strategies to offer children reading experiences such as group reading, paired reading and taped books, a higher proportion of the effective teachers reported using silent reading, reading games, reading in role play, reading environmental print and browsing among a range of books. As many of these teachers stated in a previous section of the questionnaire that children need to know that print carries meaning, know the features and directionality of print and enjoy reading, these may be the sorts of activity used to support such beliefs.

These forty-two categories of activity were sorted into the following macro-categories:

- reading contexts
- reading text types
- sub-word and word-level activities

- sentence-level activities
- text-level activities
- critical response and evaluation activities.

The percentage of responses made by each sample in each macro-category is summarised in Table 3.3. The figures suggest that while both groups offered activities involving a range of reading formats and activities at a word and sub-word level, the effective teachers offered slightly more activities that provided a reading context and slightly fewer sentence-level activities. This suggests again that the priority for this group of effective teachers of literacy seemed to be the provision of meaningful and motivating contexts in which they could teach children the essential skills of reading.

This pattern was confirmed by observations of classroom activity. The effective teachers we observed usually asked children to read whole texts in a variety of settings. However, as part of this work they placed emphasis on particular aspects of the texts, including structural features, vocabulary, word attack strategies, extracting information and enjoyment. The effective teachers were able to identify clearly their teaching purpose for children reading a text and also to identify what they wanted children to learn from reading that text. The teachers in the validation sample were more likely to be less clear about their teaching purposes, the desired learning outcomes, or both.

The questionnaire results suggested a low incidence of activities at sentence level. However, evidence from classroom observation suggests that it was not the case that the effective teachers were ignoring sentence-level work but rather that they preferred to teach about sentences and aspects of grammar through an initial focus on reading or writing a whole text. Although the effective teachers were teaching about sentence structure, they were less likely to highlight it as the overall aim of a lesson.

Table 3.3 Categories of reading activity used

Reading activities: macro-categories	Effective teachers mentioning this (%)	Validation teachers mentioning this (%)
Reading contexts	59.4	54.2
Reading formats	15.5	15.0
Sub-lexical and lexical activities	12.2	13.3
Sentence-level activities	2.5	5.8
Text-level activities	5.6	3.3
Critical response and evaluation activities	4.1	5.0

An example of this is Mrs G, who taught a poetry writing lesson to a Year 3 class. A major focus of this lesson was the use of adjectives to describe images of winter, which was the focus of the poetry session. To define these she drew up lists of things you might see on a winter day (nouns) and words that described these things (adjectives). When asked about the literacy content of the session, she said that it was a session to teach adjectives in the setting of writing a poem. She had chosen to do this to build upon work on nouns that the children had completed and intended this session to clarify the difference between the roles of nouns and adjectives. However, the aim of her lesson as indicated in her planning was 'poetry writing'. Like the majority of the effective teachers, she had embedded the teaching of specific language features within a wider writing activity. This was less noticeable in the teaching of the validation sample, who tended to teach language features directly, often without providing children with a clear context in which these features served a function.

The picture again emerges of the effective teachers of literacy actively assisting their pupils to make connections between the text, sentence and word levels of literacy work. They were able to draw upon their knowledge of language to plan deliberately for these connections, a knowledge that, as we shall see later, was characterised by its functional and connected nature.

The range of writing activities used

The percentage of respondents who used the writing activities listed is summarised in Table 3.4. As with reading, the writing activities reported in the questionnaire by both the effective teachers of literacy and the validation teachers differed according to the age group they taught. The teachers of Key Stage 2 classes were more likely than the Key Stage 1 teachers to report that children wrote for audiences other than the teacher, wrote up research and edited each other's work. A greater proportion of Key Stage 1 teachers reported children doing handwriting practice, copying out words, sounding out spellings and doing letter-string exercises. This pattern was also evident in the classroom observations and may reflect several things: a developmental assumption about the sort of work children are capable of; the need for younger children to focus on a range of basic skills to enable them to make a start with reading and writing; or the ability of older children to write more sustained texts.

The effective teachers of literacy reported more often than the validation teachers that they had used letter-string exercises, interactive writing and writing for an audience other than the teacher. Classroom observations confirmed this. The effective teachers also reported less use of published materials and children copying out words written by the teacher. In the lessons observed, the effective teachers at Key Stage 1 used published materials to consolidate points already taught, whereas the validation sample were more likely to use them to introduce a teaching point.

Table 3.4 Writing activities reported as being used by teachers

Teaching activity	Effective KS 1 teachers reporting use of this (%)	Validation KS 1 teachers reporting use of this (%)	Effective KS 2 teachers reporting use of this (%)	Validation KS 2 teachers reporting use of this (%)
Letter formation/handwriting	97.6	90.3	79.0	76.1
Copying words written by the teacher	52.0	54.8	23.0	39.1
Sounding out spellings	66.4	71.0	47.0	45.7
Children doing letter-string exercises	46.4	35.5	40.0	30.4
Writing news/personal views	68.8	67.7	65.0	54.3
Writing on a topic chosen by children	65.6	45.2	40.0	47.8
Writing for an audience other than the teacher	80.0	64.5	86.0	73.9
Writing frames	26.4	25.8	36.0	28.3
Writing after a piece of research	34.4	29.0	69.0	71.7
Peer group editing	12.8	22.6	56.0	39.1
Using published English materials	25.6	45.2	41.0	43.5
Interactive writing	41.6	32.3	44.0	34.8

In both reading and writing, the effective teachers of literacy were able to provide a wider range of literacy-teaching activities that emphasised using whole texts as a setting for learning about literacy. They were also less reliant on decontextualised exercises, deriving most of their teaching of sentence and word features from these whole texts.

When asked about other writing activities used, the effective teachers reported using forty-three other writing activities, whereas the validation teachers reported thirty-one. Of these activities, the most frequently mentioned are summarised in Table 3.5. It is notable that a great many of these categories refer to particular forms of writing. The effective teachers were much more likely to report writing in role play, writing lists, writing instructions, collaborative writing and modelling or scribing for children. The validation teachers reported more reports/descriptions and spelling skills activities.

The macro-categories derived from this list of writing activities were as follows:

Table 3.5 Other writing activities reportedly used

Writing teaching activity	Effective teachers mentioning this (%)	Validation teachers mentioning this (%)
Writing cards, letters and postcards	28.4	17.4
Writing poems	21.0	17.4
Writing in role play/play	17.6	4.3
Lists	13.1	6.5
Reports and descriptions	11.4	28.3
Book or newspaper making	11.4	13.0
Scripts/jokes	10.8	10.9
Collaborative writing	10.2	6.5
Note making/precis	9.1	8.7
Computer use	6.8	6.5
Instructions	5.7	0.0
Teacher scribing/modelling	5.7	0.0
Spelling skills	3.5	19.6
Dictionary exercises	4.0	2.2
Word games	4.0	2.2
Comprehension and short answers	4.0	4.3

- **forms of writing**: such as writing letters or labels;
- **contexts for writing**: such as writing in role play or collaborative writing;
- **word-level activities**: such as alphabet games or vocabulary study;
- **sentence-level activities**: such as text marking or grammar exercises;
- **text-level activities**: such as studying bias in writing or reviewing stories.

The percentage of responses made by each sample in each macro-category is summarised in Table 3.6.

The distribution of these activities was broadly similar across the two groups, although the effective teachers reported a greater proportion of activities that provided contexts for writing, such as group composition or revising writing with a partner, and the validation teachers reported a greater proportion of word-level (principally spelling) activities. Both groups were alike in terms of the priority they seemed to place upon finding a range of forms in which children could write.

The classroom observations certainly confirmed that the effective teachers offered clearer contexts for the literacy activities they set. They generally took pains to relate tasks to work already completed, to explain the purpose

Table 3.6 Categories of writing activity used

Writing activities: macro-categories	Effective teachers mentioning this (%)	Validation teachers mentioning this (%)
Forms of writing	62.4	63.0
Contexts for writing	15.4	8.7
Word-level activities	9.1	15.2
Sentence-level activities	2.0	2.2
Text-level activities	10.6	9.8

of the knowledge to be taught, and to relate the texts used to topics of class study.

We were particularly interested in the use of sentence-level activities. Although both groups of teachers *reported* using few activities explicitly targeted at sentence-level knowledge, we found in our observations that, compared with the validation sample, the effective teachers were equally, or more, likely to focus on sentence-level aspects of text in lessons. The ways in which both groups did this differed. The effective teachers tended to work on aspects of sentence grammar or punctuation in the context of the writing of whole texts and to show explicitly how that aspect of grammar contributed to meaning. The validation teachers tended to offer exercises that aimed to study only a particular aspect of sentence-level grammar out of context. We made a similar point in the earlier section on reading activities, and its replication here suggests a common pattern.

As an example of this phenomenon, we give below a description of a lesson taught by Mrs J, a Key Stage 2 effective teacher.

Mrs J said the aim of her session was to teach the children in her class to write dialogue using the conventions of inverted commas and punctuation and to link this with the characters in the class novel.

She started the session by reading a passage from *The Demon Headmaster*, which included dialogue and used the appropriate conventions. The children followed the passage in shared copies of the text. She then used the blackboard to ask children questions about how this passage of direct speech was set out. She introduced the terms dialogue, inverted comma, comma, capital letter and speaker and asked children to define them and offer reasons why they were used that way. The class then collectively invented the rest of the dialogue, which she wrote on the blackboard with the children supplying the conventions and telling her how to place them. Most of the children volunteered information, but Mrs J chose a few children to whom she directed particular questions. This introduction took less than 20 minutes.

Mrs J then asked the children to work in pairs to write a dialogue between any two characters in the book. She said the dialogue had to reflect the personalities of the characters chosen and to be appropriately set out. The class had 20 minutes to complete the task and would then be performing their short dialogues for the other class members. As the children worked Mrs J went to work with three pairs of children in particular, one of whom she asked to work on the word processor. She spent approximately 10 minutes with these children, then walked around the class asking questions and offering help. The children worked industriously and appeared to feel the pressure of time upon them. Mrs J warned the children when there was 5 minutes to go and then stopped the class.

The pairs of children performed their dialogues. For each pair Mrs J commented on the way the words and intonation reflected the personality of the character and asked questions about the way they had set out the dialogue on paper. She checked their scripts as they handed them in. The children clearly enjoyed the activity and took her praise and pointers seriously.

The whole lesson took less than an hour. Following the lesson, Mrs J briefly reported the children's level of attainment. She felt that the groups she had worked with were still unsure about the capital letter conventions for breaking an utterance, while the other children had generally mastered this aspect of the activity. She would be able to check this when she marked the scripts. In doing so she would look for use of inverted commas, commas, capital letters, new lines and appropriate choice of content.

It is notable here that Mrs J taught the use of inverted commas in the context of the class novel and took care to emphasise the function of written dialogue, rather than simply the rules for writing it. She was able to teach sentence-level knowledge explicitly within the setting of a meaningful text, thus helping her pupils to make vital connections between these two levels of knowledge. Again, this ability to make connections between two or more levels was characteristic of the effective teachers of literacy but not of the validation teachers. The effective teachers were able to draw upon their functional knowledge of language to plan deliberately for these connections.

Task presentation and lesson structure

The lessons of the effective teachers that we observed were characterised by a very brisk pace. A single school session (approximately a quarter of a school day) usually contained two or more tasks. These teachers were, in effect, generally teaching a daily literacy hour, even if this was not always of the exact format implicit in the National Literacy Strategy.

The effective teachers of literacy tended to refocus the attention of their children on the literacy task at regular points in the session. They also made regular checks on children's progress and frequently asked children to provide examples of work in progress, either for the teacher to comment on or for the whole class to hear or comment upon. Such activities were rarely observed in the validation classes.

The use of time in effective teachers' classes was also closely monitored, with teachers setting time limits for particular sub-tasks, such as planning, within the larger task, such as writing the beginning of the story. It was notable that this behaviour characterised not only the Key Stage 2 classes but even the reception classes, where the children were unlikely to have a well-developed sense of time. We concluded that the effective teachers of literacy were using this tactic to induct their reception children into patterns of working that included focusing on a task and pushing themselves to complete it.

The beginnings and conclusions of sessions for groups and classes taught by the effective teachers had a number of distinct characteristics. In addition to clear focus and functional discussion, effective literacy teachers were observed using modelling extensively. They used blackboards, flipcharts, posters and whiteboards to demonstrate not only what was to be produced in a lesson but also the processes involved. They were observed to do the following:

- write dialogue
- write letters to fantasy characters
- skim and scan texts while describing their own thought processes
- write letters and collect words beginning with those letters
- make notes
- demonstrate intonation in reading aloud
- sing nursery rhymes, emphasising rhyme
- select words from Breakthrough folders
- model formal and informal speech
- punctuate text;

and many other similar activities.

These acts offered their children insights into how literacy tasks were achieved as well as into what the aims of the tasks were. Models of thought in planning, drafting, correcting writing, making decisions, sounding out words and using dictionaries also punctuated the lessons of the effective teachers.

One reception teacher told us a little about why she modelled writing for her class.

'I noticed when you demonstrated writing you talked about the capital letters, the pronoun I and exclamation marks. Why?'

'Its something I do from the day they arrive at school. I demonstrate writing. I talk about what is happening on the flipchart and they begin to pick up adult conventions without a "formal" lesson. It's our every-day approach.'

'Do you do it often?'

'Oh yes, whenever I am demonstrating, not just in writing. I am always talking about the conventions of writing and what I am doing and I feel they are learning an awful lot more if they realise that it is just part of writing and reading. When they are reading to me we discuss where the full stops come and commas and speech marks. I am trying to train them to an awareness of everything so that if they question they will learn. But if no one points things out to them they might not even ask.'

Both the effective teachers of literacy and the validation teachers used a wide range of questions. However, the effective teachers more frequently asked children how they accomplished tasks, how they made literacy decisions, what reading cues they used, and to explain conclusions and comprehension decisions. The following exchange, for instance, was observed in one Key Stage 2 teacher's lesson:

'How do you know he doesn't mean it?'

'It says so in the book.'

'What part? What tells you that?'

'It says here [points to the book] ". . . he said, laughing wickedly". It means that he says so, but he doesn't mean it. And he's like that, isn't he? I mean, from what sort of person he is. He isn't going to help really I don't think.'

'So you think that it's the way he laughs as he says it and what you know about him that tell you he doesn't mean it.'

'Yes.'

'He's lying then?'

Another Key Stage 2 teacher discussed a child's choice of word for a cloze passage in the following way:

'Why did you put in "tumbled" there then?'

'Well, it fitted.'

'How did you know?'

'I read the whole bit. To ". . . right by the shore line." and then went back and thought "a something down shack right by the shore line". It might be fallen. But it might be tumbled down, like in fairy stories. It's a bit like that.'

'So reading over the gap you found a word to fit in. Well done. I like it.'

A Key Stage 1 teacher was observed writing her 'news' for the children and asking them questions about her own writing.

'I went to . . . Well where?'
Children call out: 'Cinema? Shops? Supermarket?'
'Yes, the supermarket. Do I put it here?' [positions pen at extreme right of flipchart]
Children call out: 'no, other side, down.'
'On the other side? And the next line? Why, why can't I start here?'
Children call out: 'it won't fit, the word won't fit, you need a new line.'
'OK on the new line so that we can read along and down. Supermarket begins with?'
Children call out: 's,(s)'
'Yes (s) is the sound and the letter is called?'
Children call out: 's'
'Yes "s" for supermarket.' [Sounds out as she writes] 's oo p er - m ar k et. All together.' [all join in as she points]. 'I went to the supermarket. It's the new Safeway I went to. Who's been?'

These types of question in whole class or group lessons were largely confined to the effective teachers and emphasise their concern for raising children's awareness of their own literacy use and comprehension. The use of these questions in whole class and group sessions led children into thinking about what they are reading or writing at a very high level and offered them models of strategy use and comprehension. All the effective teachers that we observed reading individually with their children asked these types of question during individual reading interactions. Such questions are referred to in current learning theory as 'scaffolding' and act as supports that help children to think at a higher level than they would be capable of if left entirely alone.

The lessons of the effective teachers of literacy were also likely to be concluded by a review of the tasks accomplished or by the teacher asking the children to present a report or extracts of their work. Such 'plenary' lesson conclusions are, of course, characteristic of the National Literacy Strategy literacy hour structure.

The classes of the effective teachers generally concluded the task assigned during the observed lessons. When this was not the case, the teachers gave a clear indication of when the task would be concluded. At Key Stage 2, there was a marked contrast between this and the validation sample teachers, who were more likely to expect children to hand in work for subsequent marking without teacher comment or 'rounding up'. In a number of the validation teachers' lessons that we observed, the teachers asked some children to 'finish off later' but did not specify when. This gave these lessons a very much less obvious structure.

High levels of engagement with the literacy tasks were also noted in the effective teachers' classes, possibly reflecting the careful focusing by teachers and the academic pressure resulting from a brisk pace and active monitoring of pupil performance.

Differentiation of content and tasks

The ways teachers differentiated the content of lessons for different children naturally had implications for the ways they organised their class activity. A number of arrangements were observed, and some patterns emerged.

Teachers were asked during post-lesson interviews: 'Was the content of that session different for different children?'. In a small proportion of the lessons of both the validation group and the effective teachers, the teacher had set different tasks for different children, depending on their perceived needs. In the classes of the effective teachers, examples observed included individualised spelling tests in which children tested each other, and individual reading, where books were matched to a child's perceived abilities.

However, in most classes teachers offered the same literacy content for all their children, although this did not necessarily mean that all children did the same task at the same time. There were a range of ways in which the work undertaken was differentiated for pupils. Overwhelmingly, this took account of the children's abilities as perceived by the teacher. In some cases, mostly in the lessons of the validation sample, teachers said that they differentiated the outcomes of the session, in that they had different expectations for different pupils. Such differential expectations were not necessarily evident to the researcher or to the children. In the classes of the effective teacher's this approach was observed during routine individual activities such as silent reading, and reading 'carousel' activities (a reading carousel is a system in which the teacher organises several reading tasks for her class, allocates these to specific groups for part of a lesson, and then rotates groups through the tasks).

A much more frequently observed pattern in the classes of the effective teachers was for teachers to set the same task for all the children but to vary deliberately the amount of support they gave to the children to help them to achieve the learning target. The support given included offering much more detailed instructions on sheets, work cards and posters, and offering scaffolding devices such as writing frames. It also included teachers or classroom assistants working with particular (not always the least able) groups, and offering transcription help for writers (scribing or using the computer). For example, in one Year 3 lesson the children were asked to write a letter to their future teachers to introduce themselves. The task and the required product was the same for all the children: indeed, the whole school would be doing this task at some time, to help the teachers get to know their future classes. Miss L gave the whole class an introduction in which she explained not only why the letters would be useful to the writer and recipient but also examined the features of a sample letter. The class then divided into four seating groups and began to work on individual drafts. One group received little support, apart from notes made on a whiteboard during the whole class introduction. The second group was referred to a poster about the features of a letter and the main points emphasised. The other two groups used a 'writing frame' with questions to focus the content and language of the lesson. The teacher herself spent most of the lesson working alongside the least able members of the class.

One teacher mentioned the effect on her planning of offering this differential support:

> It depends what the activity is. I say I would probably, if it is particularly, you know, a teaching point, I may well have to work with one group and stay with them and plan accordingly, so that the other groups are much more self-contained where they are not going to need as much support. I tend to introduce things to the whole class and then we split into groups.

This approach to differentiating the teaching of literacy to meet the perceived needs of the children was organised in a number of ways. In Key Stage 2 classes, children were most likely to all work individually on the same task at the same time. In Key Stage 1 classes, teachers also organised tasks so that different groups did them at different times, presumably to organise the use of the teacher's time. In one reception class, for example, one of the teacher's literacy aims for the day she was observed was to introduce her class to the structure of a recipe, as an example of the instructional genre. (The class had made cakes the previous week and had followed a recipe written out by the teacher.) She organised her class into activity groups, with some help from classroom assistants and volunteer parents. During the lesson observed, she worked first with a group of the least able children, who had not yet really made a start at reading and writing. With this group, she talked about how they had made their cakes and showed them some recipe books. They discussed items like the list of ingredients and the pictures of the things to be cooked. The session ended with the teacher scribing as the children told her the ingredients they had used to make their cakes. The class then rotated to different activities and the teacher worked with a much more able group. She covered essentially the same content with them, but these children were asked to begin writing their cake recipes for themselves using the structure she had shown them.

Classroom literacy environments

The influence of the classroom environment on the successful development of literacy has been well established in a number of research studies.

During our classroom observations for this project, we took note of the literacy environments provided in these classrooms. We also tried to focus in our observations on the children's response to these environments. Three main qualities characterised the literacy environments of the effective teachers of literacy: presence, function and use by children.

Presence

Although in most of the classes we observed we could see evidence of the teacher's efforts to provide appropriate resources for literacy learning, much more priority was clearly given to this in the classes of the effective teachers. These teachers had also made efforts to draw the children's attention to the features and functions of literacy. Their classes featured resources such as alphabet friezes, word banks, displays of books at an appropriate age level, displays of books related to the topic under consideration, listening centres, reference books, reading scheme books, language master machines, word games and computers (although only one instance of computer use was seen). These resources were not always new, and the teachers had clearly drawn on a range of sources, including school resources, materials brought in by children, schools library services and a museum service. Their classrooms were labelled with the names of areas, drawers and containers, injunctions to use the resources and instructions for looking up words, revising text, editing text, selecting books, changing library books, using dictionaries and using mnemonics. Work by pupils was displayed, usually, but not always, at child eye level.

While many of these items are a normal part of the primary classroom at Key Stage 1 and 2, they were very much more in evidence in the classes of the effective teachers than in the classes of the validation teachers. However, the functions and use of these items also particularly distinguished the classes of the effective teachers of literacy.

Function

Most of the items in the effective teachers' classes had a clear function. There were, for instance, posters instructing children about aspects of writing, posters and leaflets about using dictionaries or libraries, labels to assist children in finding resources, 'flashes' with notices attracting attention to new materials or displays, and suggestion boxes. These were in sharp contrast to the much less functional displays in the validation classes, where it was more common to see displays of children's work used purely to decorate classroom walls but with no obvious link to current reading and writing work being done in the class.

Use by children

The effective teachers were observed directing children's attention to the literacy items on display and using them as a support strategy for particular groups of children undertaking tasks. Children were observed using instructions to perform reading and writing tasks such as using 'the five-finger' test (a simple readability measure) from a wall poster to select a reading book, using an index of the Dewey library system to select an information book, looking through a 'mini-beasts' word bank for a word to use in their writing, using a laminated alphabet card to 'sound out' a spelling, and using a 'language master' machine to check an unknown spelling. This may be a reflection of purely organisational strategies to allow primary-age readers and writers a degree of independence. However, the effect of it was to make reading and the use of text essential activities in these classrooms.

In some Key Stage 1 classes (especially those with younger children), dramatic play areas included a high literacy content, reflecting our questionnaire finding that the effective teachers reported much more writing in role play. Books, newspapers, directories, paper, forms and posters were provided as a part of dramatic play. For instance, in one reception class, groups of children playing in the 'post office' wrote letters to friends, filled in forms and sorted parcels, while other groups of children completed more 'formal' literacy tasks. No direct comparison was made between these situations and those provided by the validation teachers as none of the validation classes included dramatic play areas.

Assessment and monitoring of literacy tasks

The questionnaire completed by both the effective teachers and the validation teachers enquired into their use of a variety of approaches to the assessment of literacy development. Teachers' use of assessment approaches were also a focus of the classroom observations and subsequent interviews.

Assessment strategies reported

Respondents to the questionnaire were asked to indicate against a list of approaches to the assessment of literacy whether and how often they used these. The summaries of their responses are given in Table 3.7. The figures represent the percentages of each group of teachers who said they used that approach either a great deal or quite often.

We did know that the schools in which the effective teachers taught administered standardised reading tests (this was one of the bases on which these teachers were selected). The questionnaire results, however, suggested that the effective teachers of literacy were less likely than the validation teachers to place reliance upon tests for their assessment in literacy. They were more likely to use assessment techniques such as marking, error

Table 3.7 Assessment strategies reportedly used by teachers

Assessment strategy	Effective teachers reporting use of this (%)	Validation teachers reporting use of this (%)
Teacher-made tests	39.9	46.5
Tests from published schemes	7.0	19.8
Standardised tests	14.5	19.7
Marking written products	53.1	47.9
Miscue analysis	26.7	12.7
Running records	58.8	55.0
Observation of children	93.2	84.5
Children's self-assessment	51.7	33.8

analysis and observation. It may be that these teachers regarded stan-dardised tests as having other purposes beyond directly informing their teaching, such as monitoring standards from year to year. One teacher, talking about her use of tests, commented:

> [Standardised tests give a] good indication of where the child is at, but it's not very diagnostic. It doesn't help me point out where the problems are. The SATs test is actually much more diagnostic in the way that it throws up what the specific problems are. I think to use one [a test] that was more diagnostic would just take up so much time, which obviously, we haven't got to spend on an individual basis.

In the questionnaire, teachers were also asked to name other approaches to the assessment of literacy that they used and that were not included in the list given. A further fifty-five approaches were added by the effective teachers of literacy. These included such ideas as 'reading conferences' (mentioned by 20 per cent of those responding), analysis of samples of writing (15.6 per cent), use of statement banks (11.1 per cent), peer assessment (11.1 per cent), moderation (8.9 per cent) and alphabet recognition (8.9 per cent). Only three validation group teachers wrote anything here, two adding 'reading conferences' and one 'baseline assessment', reinforcing the pattern of their more intensive use of a narrower range of approaches.

Assessment strategies observed

A number of the monitoring and assessment strategies mentioned in the questionnaires were observed in lessons taught by effective teachers of literacy, including recording pupils' use of reading and writing strategies, noting pupils' enjoyment of group and individual reading, discussing reading diaries with children, marking work in progress, returning marked work, asking children how they had achieved a task or taken a decision, asking children to provide further examples, and taking reports of group and individual reading from assistants and parent helpers.

Some of the effective teachers appeared to monitor the whole class by walking around looking at work in progress and questioning individual pupils or groups. This, however, was a minority activity more often seen in the validation teachers' lessons at Key Stage 2. More usually, the effective teachers worked particularly closely with one group of children, probing, questioning and supporting, and made intermittent 'rounds' of the class to observe the activities of the children. The 'conclusions' of the lessons already described, in which children read out or discussed samples of work, also offered teachers an opportunity to monitor children's progress.

Teachers were asked during interviews how they monitored or assessed the lesson observed. The answers of the effective teachers were surprisingly consistent. Almost all cited observation as their chief tool in assessment and gave examples of their observations about particular children.

> Well, observation assessment, clearly. The teacher is so engaged in moving around and doing that you can only assess by observation in that situation. What I'll do now, or even tonight, is in my planning and assessment folder. That's together. I'll make comments on various children. So I just have a child's name at the top of each sheet of paper and I put down, a sense that's only the teacher's log, I won't make a comment on every child, that's not possible, and I would never say to you that it is possible, because that puts pressure on other people. But over the year I will make observations on every child several times.

Many of the teachers went on to describe their methods of recording these observations:

> Well we have a tick sheet for their letter sounds which I go through per-haps once every few weeks at the moment to check they can still say their sounds. So that is formal assessment, but I keep a tick sheet of their work that they've finished. For the writing we have an evaluation and I record that on their termly record card.

> Well, the first record we keep is the pre-reading skills that I fill in after about half a term from my notes. That's the first one. I chat with parents about it at the first Open Night . . . after that I move off onto sight words and make a summative record 'Knows the first 20 words' and sign and date it.

> I have a written summary of what's happened in a group reading session. That's what's in the . . . , I have a group reading record book,

which is divided into six groups, for my ability groups and the mum who is reading with them will record, basically, how well the child read, whether they were interested, whether they took an active part in discussion. Well, they have the chart of fifteen questions and teaching points about the group reading to discuss: title, author, ISBN, characters, you know. So I get a written summary from that.

Most of the effective teachers also mentioned other assessment techniques, including discussion with children and records of individual reading and inspection of writing products.

The assessment and recording emphasis for the effective teachers appeared to be slightly different for reading and writing tasks. All the teachers told us about individual reading records that were kept continuously with the involvement of parents and helpers, and sometimes children. In writing, they reported keeping a collection of examples and using National Curriculum levels to make periodic judgements about these.

Where teachers discussed their use of records there were two main emphases: periodic checks on the progress of children; and the setting of future targets on the basis of the evidence collected:

Say, every half term I have a look and glance back at what they've done, then I write what I think they need. Unless, sometimes, it might be obvious what she needs to work on, in fact that word 'went' I'm going to reinforce a bit with her, so I might write that down. But usually I do what they need next every half term.

I have got to teach those children something. Whatever I do those children have got to be learning something. So I know where those children are in the scheme of things and I know what they need to get out of a particular session. It's just knowing what you have to do with them.

It is really for, to show you where a child is and what he can do and any significant changes in reading behaviour. Also if the head wants to know where a child is, say every half term.

These attitudes to assessment contrasted with the responses from the validation teachers. A number of these said that they had not assessed at all during the lessons observed and cited future occasions on which those skills or abilities would be assessed. There was more concern with assessing against a class target rather than an individual approach. This suggests that the teachers in the validation sample were likely to be more concerned with discrete skills and the meeting of class targets, whereas the effective teachers placed more emphasis upon identifying and developing the skills of individual children and saw assessment as enabling them to do this.

Summary

This summary of our findings concerning the teaching practices of the effective teachers of literacy does suggest some important features of effective teaching. These can be summarised as follows:

- There were some differences between the reading activities likely to be employed by the effective teachers and the teachers in the validation group. The effective teachers made more use of big books in their teaching; they were also more likely to use other adults to assist their classroom work. The validation teachers made more use of phonic exercises and flashcards, although both groups were similar in the extent to which they reported and were observed to teach letter sounds. The difference was in the ways they went about this. The effective teachers tended to teach letter sounds within the context of using a text (often a big book) and to use short, regular teaching sessions, often involving them modelling to the children how sounds worked (by, for example, writing examples of letter groups on a flipchart). The validation teachers were much more likely to approach letter sound teaching through the use of paper exercises.
- The effective teachers were generally much more likely to embed their teaching of reading into a wider context. They tended to use whole texts as the basis from which to teach skills such as vocabulary, word attack and recognition and use of text features. They were also very clear about their purposes for using such texts.
- In lessons involving writing the differences between the two groups of teachers were less clear, although it did seem that the effective teachers were more likely to use published teaching materials as a way of consolidating the language points they had already taught their children, whereas for the validation teachers, these materials were often used to introduce a teaching session. This suggests that a similar point to that made about reading work also applies in the case of writing work. The effective teachers generally tried to ensure that their teaching of language features was contextualised for their children and that the children understood the purpose of this teaching. Their chief means of achieving such contextualisation was to focus teaching on a shared text. Language features were taught, and explained to the children, as a means of managing this shared text rather than as a set of rules or definitions to be learned for their own sakes.
- The effective teachers of literacy, because of their concern to contextualise their teaching of language features within shared text experiences, made explicit connections for their pupils between the text, sentence and word levels of language study.
- The lessons of the effective teachers were all conducted at a brisk pace. They regularly refocused children's attention on the task at hand and

used clear time frames to keep children on task. They also tended to con-clude their lessons by reviewing, with the whole class, what the children had done during the lesson. Lessons that ended with the teacher simply saying 'We'll finish this tomorrow' were much more common among the validation teachers.

- The effective teachers used modelling extensively. They regularly demonstrated reading and writing to their classes in a variety of ways, often accompanying these demonstrations by verbal explanations of what they were doing. In this way, they were able to make available to the children their thinking as they engaged in literacy.

- Some effective teachers differentiated the work they asked pupils to do by allotting different tasks on the basis of ability. However, these teachers also used another approach to differentiation by varying the support given to particular groups of children when they were engaged on tasks that the whole class would do at some point. By this means, they were able to keep their classes working more closely together through a programme of work.

- The classrooms of the effective teachers were distinguished by the heavy emphasis on literacy in the environments that had been created. Many examples of literacy were displayed in these classrooms, these examples were regularly brought to the children's attention, and the children were encouraged to use them to support their own literacy.

- The effective teachers had very clear assessment procedures, usually involving a great deal of focused observation and systematic record keeping. This contributed markedly to their abilities to select appro-priate literacy content for their children's needs.

4   The subject knowledge of effective teachers of literacy

Introduction

A central hypothesis of this research was that there would be a clear relationship between effectiveness in teaching literacy and teachers' subject knowledge in literacy. However, defining subject knowledge in literacy is by no means simple. In this chapter, we will discuss ways of defining literacy subject knowledge before presenting our findings concerning the subject knowledge that appeared to underpin the effective teachers of literacy in our study.

Subject knowledge in teaching literacy

In Chapter 1, we reviewed some of the evidence that suggests that effective teachers of a number of subjects tend to possess a well-developed knowledge base in those subjects. Such a knowledge base appears to consist of knowledge about content, knowledge about children and their learning and knowledge about how to teach the subject effectively. It has not yet, however, been established that effective teachers of literacy are in a similar position with regard to their 'subject'.

An important point to make here is to stress the difference between English as a school subject and literacy. There is evidence that the subject knowledge of specialist English teachers (at secondary level) is specific, well developed and largely literature-focused (Poulson *et al.*, 1996). But teachers of literacy are not necessarily English subject specialists. The effective teachers of literacy studied in this research, although more likely to have an English subject background than teachers in the validation sample, were not highly qualified in English – 66.7 per cent of them had an A level in English or a related subject, but only 37.8 per cent had pursued this subject to degree level. Literacy is not in fact a 'subject' in the usual sense, with clearly defined boundaries and conventions. Its content draws upon a number of disciplines, including the psychology of learning, child language development, linguistics and literary criticism and is best expressed as a series of interlinking processes rather than a body of knowledge.

In defining subject knowledge in literacy, therefore, we were forced to extrapolate from more general studies of subject knowledge and used a three-part model as a starting point for our analysis. Subject knowledge in literacy, we felt, could be considered as broadly consisting of three connected but distinct components:

1   knowledge of literacy content and functions, i.e. what children need to learn in literacy in order to be counted as successful;
2   pedagogical content knowledge, i.e. how the content and processes of literacy can be represented and taught successfully to children;
3   knowledge about learners and the ways in which they learn, i.e. how children learn to read, write and use language effectively, and what the capabilities are of the pupils currently being taught?

Content knowledge in teaching literacy

The most problematic of the above was content knowledge, and defining this in literacy did not prove easy. Content in literacy covers both knowledge (e.g. knowledge of literature, knowledge of the linguistic system) and skills. Literacy teachers teach children *how to* read and write as well as *about* reading and writing. Success in literacy is measured not by what children know about texts, print, etc. but by what they can do in literacy.

A further issue for teacher's content knowledge is that although all primary teachers are effective readers and writers and have demonstrated this through examination success, they learned these skills without necessarily becoming explicitly aware of them. The degree to which an awareness of one's own language use is necessary is a very problematic issue that has long been discussed by authors such as Kavanagh and Mattingley (1972).

For this project, we began by defining content knowledge as including knowledge of the following elements of literacy:

• the use and function of word- and sub-word-level aspects of language (phonics, spelling and vocabulary) and the relationship of these to other levels of language;
• the use and function of sentence-level aspects of language (grammar and punctuation) and the relationship of these to other levels of language;
• the use and function of text-level aspects of language (comprehension and composition) and the relationships between these;
• the use, function and relationships of text types and texts (range and purpose).

A more detailed description of the components of these elements was given in Chapter 1.

The evidence from our study suggests that the effective teachers of literacy used a limited range of content knowledge but did so in characteristic ways, suggesting that their knowledge was functional and context-specific. The study also produced some evidence that effective teachers' content knowledge could not readily be separated from their pedagogical content knowledge. The knowledge appeared to exist for teachers in the ways in which they operationalised it for their pupils. Teachers may have evolved this working knowledge from a theoretical content base, but the way it was manifested was through their use of it in teaching.

The project used a range of methods to investigate teachers' subject knowledge in literacy:

- In the initial questionnaire, we asked teachers what children needed to know about literacy at key points in their learning.
- We administered a test of literacy knowledge ('the literacy quiz') to both sub-samples of effective teachers and validation teachers.
- We observed these teachers teaching literacy lessons. The explicit focus of one round of such observations was the literacy content being taught.
- We interviewed the teachers about this literacy content at the conclusion of the lessons.

What do children need to know?

In the initial questionnaire, teachers were asked to state what they thought children needed to know about reading and writing at two points in their development: when they first encountered literacy; and at the beginning of Key Stage 2 of the National Curriculum. The purpose of these questions was to gain some insight into what the teachers knew about reading and writing through their views of what children should know.

The responses were analysed by creating categories. First, all the responses that seemed to say the same sort of thing were grouped together. For instance, a number of responses referred to the range of texts that children should read:

- 'to read fiction and non-fiction';
- 'to read a range of texts';
- 'that they can read non-fiction as well as fiction';
- 'to read computer screens, leaflets, etc. as well as books'.

These were grouped together as a single category: 'to read a range of texts'.

In this way, fifty-one separate categories were derived from responses about children's knowledge of reading and sixty-four from responses about their knowledge of writing. By carrying out a frequency analysis, we were able to derive a picture of the knowledge that the effective and validation teachers thought was important for children first encountering literacy and for children who have reached the Key Stage 2 level.

Table 4.1 Teachers' views about what children need to learn when beginning reading

What children need to learn when they first encounter reading	Effective teachers mentioning this (%)	Validation teachers mentioning this (%)
Reading is enjoyable	23.1	15.9
Books/words carry meaning	14.7	9.3
Directionality and print awareness	6.2	7.0
Phonic cues	4.7	10.3
Book structure and handling	4.6	16.2
There are different purposes for reading	4.6	4.7
Phonological awareness	4.4	16.2
Books are an imaginative experience	4.3	2.8
Sight vocabulary	2.7	9.3

Knowledge about reading

The results show some differences between teachers' ideas about the items of knowledge needed for the two ages of children and between the two groups of teachers. For children just beginning reading, the features mentioned in more than 4 per cent of responses of either group are shown in Table 4.1.

There were some differences between the two groups in the importance they seemed to attach to particular features. The effective teachers of literacy highlighted the importance of children knowing that reading is enjoyable. They were also more likely to mention that children should realise that text carries meaning and should be aware that print is structured in particular ways, for example, running from left to right. The validation teachers had a different order of priorities, emphasising specific knowledge such as book structure and phonological awareness above an understanding of the purpose of different aspects of text.

This might suggest a different view of the sequence of children's learning about literacy in the two groups. The effective teachers tended to be concerned for the child just beginning reading to be motivated to read and to understand from the outset the purpose of reading. This is not to say they discounted the technical skills that children need in order to put such understanding to work; rather, they wanted children to see these skills as an important means to a significant end. The validation teachers, on the other hand, saw the first priorities in learning to read as the technical concepts – book handling and phonological awareness.

The teachers' views about what was important in reading at Key Stage 2 are shown in Table 4.2. With the exception of the enjoyment of reading,

Table 4.2 Teachers' views about what children need to learn about reading when they begin Key Stage 2

What children need to learn about reading when they begin KS2	Effective teachers mentioning this (%)	Validation teachers mentioning this (%)
Read a range of texts	11.2	8.7
Read for information/understanding	11.2	13.1
Reading is enjoyable	8.5	8.8
Skim, scan and extract information	7.5	7.7
Use reference skills	5.8	2.7
Make inferences and interpret texts	5.0	6.6
Make appropriate choices of reading material	4.9	6.0
There are different purposes for reading	4.8	3.3
Read aloud with expression and fluency	4.8	7.1
Recognise different stylistic features of text	4.2	1.1
Discuss reading with reference to the text	4.2	4.4

all these categories of response were different from those given in response to the question about beginning reading, which suggests that all these teachers were aware of developmental progression in learning. The effective teachers were slightly more likely to mention the need for children to read a range of texts but, in general, the reported priorities of both groups were quite similar. The emphasis seemed to be upon children's use of reading to learn, their use of a range of texts and their enjoyment of reading. These responses suggest a concern with the teaching of reading as a skill applicable in other curriculum areas.

To offer a clearer picture of such a large number of very detailed codes, the categories of response to this question were examined and grouped into macro-categories on the following basis:

- Responses that specified linguistic knowledge and knowledge of how it is used in reading. For example, the categories 'concept of word', 'alphabetical order/letter names' and 'directionality and print awareness' were subsumed into the macro-category 'structural knowledge about reading'.
- Responses that specified knowledge about reading purposes which children should learn. For example, the categories 'books are an imaginative experience', 'that there are a range of purposes for reading' and

'that books/words carry meaning' were grouped into the macro-category 'purposes for reading'.

- Responses expressed in terms of reading skills, such as 'to use phonic cues' and 'to use picture cues', 'to read aloud with expression and fluency', were grouped together as 'strategies and skills'.
- A number of categories, such as 'to read for understanding', 'make inferences and interpret from text' and 'skim, scan and extract information', were concerned with comprehension and comprehension skills. These were grouped together in the macro-category 'comprehension'.
- A number of categories of response, such as 'to read a range of texts', 'to make appropriate choices of reading material' and 'a range of text structures', emphasised the range of texts that children should know about in reading and were grouped as 'range of experience'.
- Finally, some responses, such as 'reading is enjoyable', 'care and respect for books' and 'confidence', were grouped together as the macro-category 'attitudes to reading'. It should be noted that the use of the term 'attitudes' here in fact refers to children's knowledge about reading. Teachers expressed their responses in this area in the form 'children should learn that reading is enjoyable', for example.

In this way, the following macro-categories, generated from the teachers' responses, were derived:

- purposes of reading
- range of experience
- strategies and skills
- comprehension
- structural knowledge about reading
- attitudes to reading.

These macro-categories seem broadly congruent with the National Curriculum emphasis on:

- **range** – including purposes of reading and range of experience;
- **key skills** – including strategies and skills and comprehension;
- **language study** – including knowledge about reading.

The percentage of responses falling into each of these macro-categories is shown in Table 4.3. These results suggest that the teachers in both samples believed that the kind of things that children needed to learn when first encountering literacy were different from their learning needs at the start of Key Stage 2. Early reading, they seemed to feel, demanded appreciation of purposes for reading, strategies and skills, appropriate attitudes to reading, and structural knowledge about reading. At Key Stage 2, the emphasis was more likely to be on comprehension, strategies and skills, and the

Table 4.3 Macro-categories of reading knowledge mentioned by each teacher group

Macro-category: reading knowledge	*Effective teachers mentioning this for beginning readers (%)*	*Validation teachers mentioning this for beginning readers (%)*	*Effective teachers mentioning this for KS2 readers (%)*	*Validation teachers mentioning this for KS2 readers (%)*
Purposes of reading	26.2	17.5	10.0	9.0
Range of experiences	2.2	1.9	25.8	28.2
Strategies and skills	19.7	32.2	20.9	20.9
Comprehension	2.7	1.9	26.7	28.8
Structural knowledge	23.6	27.0	7.4	4.5
Attitudes to reading	25.7	19.4	9.1	8.5

range of reading, with less concern about purposes of reading, attitudes and structural knowledge.

The effective teachers were more likely to suggest that children needed to know about purposes for reading and attitudes towards reading. The validation teachers made more mention of strategies and skills in beginning reading. These results suggest a greater concern among the effective teachers of literacy with the context in which skills were learned; that is, children's understandings about reading, their attitudes to it and their abilities to apply reading skills to a range of texts.

Knowledge about writing

A similar analysis to the above was carried out on teachers' responses to the question about what children needed to know about writing. For children just beginning writing, the features mentioned in more than 4 per cent of responses of both groups of teachers are displayed in Table 4.4. The effective teachers of literacy mentioned aspects of knowledge about writing (that it carries meaning, has a range of purposes and has an audience) most often. The validation teachers mentioned letter formation most often. As with reading knowledge, this suggests a different view of the starting points in teaching early writing, and the effective teachers seemed to be concerned for children to understand the purpose and role of writing from the outset so that they could, for example, see the need for technical skills such as forming legible letters as a means towards communicating meaning in writing.

For Key Stage 2, the effective teachers mentioned forty-five categories of knowledge, whereas the validation teachers mentioned thirty-five. Features mentioned in more than 4 per cent of responses of either group are shown in Table 4.5. With the exception of a concern that children should know

Table 4.4 Teachers' views about what children need to learn when beginning writing

What children need to learn when they first encounter writing	Effective teachers mentioning this (%)	Validation teachers mentioning this (%)
Writing carries meaning	10.3	10.3
Writing has a range of purposes	9.3	6.9
Writing communicates/has an audience	8.2	5.4
Letter formation	8.0	17.2
Knowledge of directionality	6.1	6.4
Pencil grip	6.0	7.9
Writing is valued	4.2	0.5

about the purposes of writing, the Key Stage 2 responses were different from those for early writing and indicate that these teachers had different concerns for different age levels.

The effective teachers mentioned writing forms and processes more than transcription elements such as spelling, punctuation and hand-writing, although these were still mentioned by a proportion of them. The validation teachers seemed to place emphasis on punctuation, handwriting

Table 4.5 Teachers' views about what children need to learn about writing when they begin Key Stage 2

What children need to learn about writing when they begin KS2	Effective teachers mentioning this (%)	Validation teachers mentioning this (%)
Widening range of purposes, forms, audiences and genres	15.8	10.9
redrafting	6.5	4.0
Purpose and audience determine form	6.4	6.8
Syntax and grammar	6.4	10.2
More complex content and vocabulary	5.8	5.7
Punctuation	6.7	11.9
Writing processes (drafting, revising, editing, publishing)	5.7	3.4
Spelling skills	4.3	4.5
Handwriting skills	4.3	8.6
Appropriate handwriting and spelling for purpose	4.2	2.3
Plot and character as stylistic devices	2.2	4.0

and grammar. Both groups were concerned with the range of writing that children should undertake.

Again, the categories of response to this question were grouped into macro-categories, on the following basis:

- A number of categories that specified knowledge about audience and purposes for writing, such as 'writing has a range of audiences', 'you can write for yourself' and 'to write to express', were grouped into the macro-category 'purposes and audiences for writing'.
- Those categories of response dealing with transcription aspects of writing, such as 'spelling skills', 'using word banks', 'letter formation' and 'pencil grip', were grouped into the macro-category 'transcription strategies and skills'.
- The categories dealing with writing processes, such as 'planning', 'revision with peers' and 'writing processes', were grouped into the macro-category 'process strategies and skills'.
- Categories concerned with elements of style, such as 'using stylistic devices' and 'using language to create a stylistic effect', were grouped into the macro-category 'stylistic strategies and skills'.
- Many teachers wrote about aspects of knowledge about writing, including categories such as 'that the written word is permanent', 'the difference between pictures and writing' and 'purpose and audience determine form'. These categories were grouped together as 'knowledge about writing'.
- Categories that included more specific knowledge about elements of writing, including 'the alphabet/letter names', 'more complex content and vocabulary' and 'punctuation', were grouped into the macro-category 'elements of writing'.
- Categories that referred to structures in writing, such as 'story structure' and 'range of forms and structures', were subsumed into the macro-category 'structure and organisation'.
- Teachers also specified attitudes that children should learn. Categories such as 'confidence', 'pride in work' and 'writing is enjoyable' were subsumed into the macro-category 'attitudes'.

The following macro-categories were thus used for further analysis:

- purposes and audiences for writing;
- transcription skills and strategies;
- process skills and strategies;
- stylistic skills and strategies;
- knowledge about writing;
- knowledge about specific elements of writing;
- structure and organisation of writing;
- attitudes to writing.

Although these macro-categories were generated from the teachers' responses, they again seem broadly congruent with the National Curriculum emphasis on:

- **range** – including purposes and audiences for writing;
- **key skills** – including strategies and skills (processes, transcription and style);
- **language study** – including knowledge about writing and its key elements and knowledge of structure and organisation.

The percentage of the responses falling into each of these macro-categories is shown in Table 4.6. These figures confirm the pattern that these teachers' ideas about what children should learn varied according to age phase. At the beginnings of writing the effective teachers mentioned knowledge about writing, including both the functions and features of writing, most often. This was followed by mentions of transcription skills and attitudes to writing. The validation teachers mentioned transcription skills more often and were less likely to mention positive attitudes to writing. At Key Stage 2, the effective teachers mentioned most the process skills of writing (redrafting, revising and planning), knowledge about particular elements of

Table 4.6 Macro-categories of writing knowledge mentioned by each teacher group

Macro-category: writing knowledge	Effective teachers mentioning this for beginning readers (%)	Validation teachers mentioning this for beginning readers (%)	Effective teachers mentioning this for KS2 readers (%)	Validation teachers mentioning this for KS2 readers (%)
Purposes and audiences for writing	17.3	16.3	17.4	15.7
Transcription skills and strategies	20.4	37.2	14.5	23.9
Process skills and strategies	2.3	2.0	18.9	10.1
Stylistic skills and strategies	0.5	0.0	4.1	4.4
Knowledge about writing	35.6	26.5	14.1	10.7
Knowledge about specific elements of writing	4.4	6.1	18.2	25.8
Structure and organisation of writing	0.8	1.5	7.6	6.3
Attitudes to writing	18.9	10.2	5.2	3.1

writing, and the audiences and purposes for writing. The validation teachers mentioned knowledge about specific elements of writing and transcription skills more.

From the evidence we gained from this section of the questionnaire, it seems that the priorities of these two groups of teachers in terms of what children should know about literacy were rather different. The effective teachers seemed to focus primarily upon children's understanding that reading and writing were meaningful processes and then on the fact that, to make these processes meaningful, technical systems for encoding and decoding meanings were vital. For the validation teachers, these priorities were more likely to be reversed.

It is important that this point is not misunderstood. It does not mean that the effective teachers discounted the importance of children learning the coding systems of literacy. We have no evidence that this was the case and, indeed, from our classroom observations of these teachers in action, they were clearly spending a lot of their teaching time focusing on these coding systems. What seems to be the case, however, is that the effective teachers strongly emphasised the functions and purposes of the codes of literacy as they taught them.

Testing teachers' content knowledge in literacy

We also collected data about teachers' knowledge of literacy through a quiz, which was administered to all the teachers we observed. (A copy of this quiz will be found in Appendix D.) We shall show that, although superficial analysis of the quiz results indicates quite low levels of performance for all teachers, the effective teachers performed better and, importantly, more quickly than the validation teachers. There are also apparently contradictory patterns in the performance of the effective teachers in elements of the quiz. They demonstrated in the classroom, for example, effective knowledge of some aspects, such as the use of phonemes, which they could show only poorly in the quiz. We will describe teachers' responses to the quiz section by section.

Knowledge of sentence parts

The first part of the quiz asked teachers to underline in a sentence words belonging to various classes: nouns, verbs, adjectives, adverbs, pronouns, conjunctions, prepositions and articles. In this way, we hoped to be able to see which teachers knew these language terms and could recognise examples of them. These basic parts of a sentence are the most likely aspects of grammar to be taught to primary-age children, so knowledge of them was likely to be important to the teachers. Our test, of course, was very brief and only tested teachers' ability to recognise an example of each word class in a sentence. The scoring system we used for this item was quite harsh:

respondents gained one mark for each example they correctly identified but had one mark deducted for each incorrect identification. We were aiming here to penalise simple guessing, but the system did result in some teachers scoring negative totals on this item.

Of a possible total score of 18, the median score for the effective teachers was 11.5, whereas the median for the validation sample was 2.5. However, much of this low validation group score was accounted for by one teacher who scored −12 on this item! Removing this teacher from the sample would improve their median score to 10.5, indicating very little real difference between the groups in terms of this knowledge. Detailed analysis showed that while all of the teachers could pick out nouns and verbs correctly, and most could pick out adjectives, the rates of success for the other items were more variable, with very low rates of success for prepositions and articles.

Word segmentation

The quiz also included a word-segmentation test, which asked teachers to segment a number of provided words into:

- syllables;
- phonemes;
- onset and rime;
- morphemes;
- sounds;
- units of meaning.

These word parts are important in the teaching of phonological awareness, phonics and some aspects of spelling so, while it was not possible to test teachers' awareness of all sub-word units, these were chosen as representative. This part of the test not only allowed us to see whether the teachers knew certain technical terms for parts of a word but also to add extra items so that we could see whether teachers were more likely to be able to segment words into sounds and meaning units, terms they would be familiar with, than phonemes and morphemes, terms that they might not know.

Of a maximum possible 22 points, the results produced a median score of 9 for the effective teachers and 10 for the validation sample. However, further investigation of these results shows that a large proportion of these scores was accounted for by the ability to break down words into syllables and pick out meaningful units within words.

Few teachers were able to complete other items effectively. Less than half of each group could segment words into onsets and rimes, and very few indeed could segment words into phonemes. One explanation for this might be that the term 'phoneme' caused the teachers some problems. It was noticeable, however, that they found the task difficult even when the better-known term 'sound' was used. Directly before completing the quiz we had observed a number of the effective teachers teaching initial and final sounds and blends in ways that were clearly successful and comprehensible to the children, so their failure on this item of the quiz was hard to explain. We shall discuss the implications of this apparent contradiction later in this chapter.

Defining language

A further part of the quiz asked the teachers to comment on a very partial, but traditionally used, definition of a verb to see whether this was understood to be partial and whether teachers could expand it. This item was chosen to indicate the teachers' levels of understanding about one of the word classes they had been asked to recognise in section 1. This item also reflected the observation that some of the validation teachers used this definition, and others like it, frequently in their classes, whereas the effective teachers were more likely to draw up functional definitions in conjunction with the children. The result was that 42.3 per cent of the effective teachers and 40 per cent of the validation teachers recognised the limitations of the definition, but only 23 per cent of the effective teachers and 10 per cent of the validation teachers attempted to expand it, all offering examples rather than using alternative linguistic definitions. This suggests that the effective teachers may have felt slightly more able to offer explanations, although not using formal linguistic terminology.

Language variation

The quiz contained two items about language variation to enable us to gain some insight into teachers' understandings about the nature and structure of standard English. We considered this important, as all teachers are required to teach primary children to use and study standard English, and the ability to do so may be related to their knowledge and ability to recognise it. The first part of the item asked teachers to define accent and dialect, the second to pick out the ways in which a transcribed piece of dialect speech differed from standard English.

Of the effective teachers, 76.9 per cent were able to name one distinguishing characteristic of accent or dialect, with only 60 per cent of the validation sample able to do this, while 88.3 per cent of the effective teachers picked out at least one way in which the spoken passage differed from standard English, compared with 60 per cent of the validation sample. However, the teachers all appeared to avoid linguistic terminology in doing so and were more likely to pick out and correct examples of the way that the dialect differed from standard English, rather than explain these differences in words.

Knowledge of children's literature

In addition to knowledge about language, we hypothesised that knowledge of children's literature would be an important part of a teacher's content knowledge. To measure teachers' familiarity with literature, including not only the recommended canon of literature but also the sort of books commonly read by children, the Children's Author Recognition Test (CART – UK), validated by Stainthorp (1996), was used. This simple test asks teachers to distinguish the names of genuine children's authors from foils in a list and offers a measure of teachers' familiarity with children's literature.

The results showed a mean score of 18.8 for the effective teachers and 15 for the validation sample (out of a possible 25). This suggests that the effective teachers had a greater level of awareness of children's authors than the validation sample.

Verbal comparisons of examples of children's writing and reading

In order to evaluate teachers' knowledge about the way that text-, sentence- and word-level knowledge about literacy might be related, the teachers were asked to compare some examples of children's writing and reading.

Writing

They were first shown two pieces of children's written work. They were asked to identify as many differences or features of the writing as they could, compare any mistakes and comment on the effectiveness of the two pieces. The pieces used were the instructions for growing cress seeds written by two children, and the teachers were all told the background to the task. The pieces were typed, to avoid difficulties with handwriting, but nothing else was corrected. Teachers' responses were taped and subsequently analysed. This involved listening to all the tapes and creating criteria grounded in the responses made. These criteria included the following categories of comment by the teachers.

SUB-WORD AND WORD-LEVEL FEATURES

- spelling
- breadth and appropriateness of vocabulary.

SENTENCE-LEVEL FEATURES

- use of sentences
- capitalisation
- tense

- imperative/declarative verbs
- temporal connectives
- use of commas and full stops.

TEXT-LEVEL FEATURES

- layout
- sequential organisation
- generic (people, you) or personal (I, we, Mrs Lewis) participants
- presence of list of ingredients
- clarity and detail of content
- reader awareness
- fitness for purpose/genre suitability.

For quantitative purposes each criterion was awarded one point, and two were awarded where a particular explanation or piece of terminology was used. Examples of all these types of response are given in Appendix D. The scores resulting from this procedure were very similar overall for both the effective teachers and the validation teachers, with medians of 10 (effective) and 9 (validation). However, these scores conceal some interesting differences in the groups' responses.

Comments about text features were very limited. Almost all the teachers did select one piece as more appropriate to the genre, but the effective teachers were much more likely to mention the importance of the list of ingredients in a set of instructions (51.5 per cent) than validation teachers (10 per cent). Also 39 per cent of the effective teachers mentioned the tense of the passage, an important genre feature, compared with just 20 per cent of the validation teachers. Very few teachers indeed (and only effective teachers) mentioned the appropriateness of the participants mentioned (*you* rather than *I* or *we*) or reader awareness.

At a word level, the effective teachers were much less likely to mention the single spelling mistake (55.4 per cent did so), whereas all the validation sample remarked on this. And 10 per cent of the effective teachers mentioned appropriate vocabulary choices, while none of the validation sample did so.

At a sentence level, almost all the teachers (93 per cent effective, 100 per cent validation) mentioned the use of capital letters, and approximately 20 per cent of both groups specifically mentioned the use of full stops, although only 11 per cent of the effective teachers, and none of the validation teachers, highlighted the use of commas. Of both teacher groups, 80 per cent mentioned sentence structure in general. However, the ways they did this raises some important questions about their knowledge of sentence structure. A large proportion of the validation teachers selected the sentences in the less effective piece of writing as 'better' because they used capital letters properly and were longer, even though they were arguably less effective in the piece of writing and less appropriate to the genre, which most teachers identified correctly. Many of these teachers also identified the first sentence of one piece as 'incorrect' because it used a capital letter incorrectly and included commas. In fact, this was the most sophisticated example of punctuation in the two pieces, correctly and appropriately using commas to punctuate a list. One possible explanation of this is that these teachers were too reliant upon a traditional (incomplete) definition of a sentence as 'something that starts with a capital letter and ends with a full stop'.

The order in which most of the two groups of teachers supplied criteria and observations was also very different. The effective teachers were more likely to mention first text-level features such as content and detail, genre, list of ingredients, etc. and then to list some of the sentence- and word-level features. Most of the teachers in the validation sample mentioned these features in the opposite order. When asked which was the more effective piece of writing for the purpose, all of the effective teachers selected the correct piece, whereas one of the validation teachers chose the narrative piece and four more initially chose this and later changed their minds as they examined the pieces more carefully.

Although the final scores were very close for the two groups, they approached the task in different ways. These results suggest that, given plenty of time to do the task and continuous prompting from an interviewer, all these teachers could generate a fairly complete list of criteria for comparing two pieces of instructional writing. However, in a busy classroom it is unlikely that teachers would spend anywhere near this length of time on passages like this, in which case the priority teachers gave to the various criteria could be very important. In the first 3–5 minutes of analysis of these writing passages, the two groups identified different criteria and made different judgements about the passages. There appeared to be a difference between teachers' *competence* in identifying and responding to language features and their *performance* under realistic conditions. In classroom conditions, with its pressing demands upon teachers' time and attention, the criteria for judging children's writing they habitually use are likely to be those that first come to their minds. If this is so, then children in the classes of teachers like those in our validation sample will be getting a quite different picture of what counts as important in writing from those with teachers like our effective teachers of literacy.

Reading

The teachers were also asked to look at two examples of children's reading to allow us to evaluate teachers' knowledge of children's cue use and comprehension strategies as well as the teachers' knowledge of important features of texts for reading. Two transcriptions of children's attempts to read and retell a version of 'The Emperor's New Clothes' were used. These were shown to the teachers, and they were asked to compare the readings, the mistakes and the features of the retellings. Their accounts were analysed by generating a list of criteria used by the teachers, which included the following.

CUE USE AND STRATEGIES

- pausing behaviour and reading fluency
- initial sound cues
- context and picture cues
- syntactic cues
- self-correction.

COMPREHENSION

- sequence of events in retelling
- relative importance of events
- degree of detail in the retelling
- predicts the story
- enjoys humour
- uses vocabulary from the reading passage in retelling
- confidence/experience
- fluency of retelling.

These criteria were awarded one point if simply referred to and two when the response was more elaborated or included appropriate terminology. Examples of all the criteria are included in Appendix D.

The results show that the effective teachers scored rather better than the validation sample, with a median score of 14.5 against 8.5. These differences in results are largely accounted for by a small number of criteria. The effective teachers were much more likely to comment in detail on the use of graphic and phonic cues at the level of initial sounds and blends. The validation teachers were just as likely to mention sounds but did so in a more general way, using expressions like 'she's OK at sounds' rather than identifying specific evidence and making inferences about particular phonic capabilities. The effective teachers were less likely to comment on pausing behaviour, but those effective teachers who did this went on to attempt to infer what the child might be doing, for instance 'it seems, from the pauses, that she's trying to read word by word, rather than looking at larger units as well'. Conversely, half of the validation teachers simply said, 'she's paused more'.

In a similar way, all the validation teachers mentioned the use of meaning cues, whereas only 84.6 per cent of the effective teachers did so. However, 30 per cent of the validation teachers simply made statements such as 'his reading makes sense', whereas only 11 per cent of the effective teachers mentioned context cues in this way, with 73 per cent pointing out the cues used and inferring the child's reading strategies from the evidence.

In considering the children's comprehension of the passages, both the effective and validation teachers mentioned most frequently the level of detail given and the child's ability to predict the story. More of the effective teachers (40 per cent, as opposed to 10 per cent of the validation group) identified items of vocabulary from the passage that the children had used in their retelling, with 30 per cent of the effective teachers using this evidence to make further inferences about the child's understanding. None of the validation teachers did this. The validation teachers commented more on the fluency of the retelling (30 per cent of validation teachers and 7 per cent of effective teachers) and the pauses in the reading, but they did not elaborate or suggest reasons for these phenomena. Half of the effective teachers mentioned the children's enjoyment of the story, whereas only 30 per cent of the validation teachers did this. In addition, 30 per cent of the effective teachers used evidence of this to infer the readers' level of experience of story. It was also notable that most of the validation teachers (70 per cent) chose to look at the reading and retellings separately, whereas 73.1 per cent of the effective teachers used the retellings and readings together and made points that drew on evidence from both sources.

The results of the analysis of the reading passages suggest that while both the effective and validation teachers were quite thorough in their evaluation of these pieces of reading, the effective teachers were likely to use more criteria and make more inferences about the children's strategies and understanding.

The effective teachers, and a few of the validation teachers, were much more able to perform well on these tasks, which demanded the generation of criteria, analysis of mistakes and inference about children's performance, than on earlier items in the literacy quiz, which lacked context. The effective teachers, in particular, made many more inferences about the children's performances on the passages and were more precise in their discussion of the evidence they used. The effective teachers also asked questions about related aspects of the children's reading and writing in different contexts and were much more likely to suggest experiences and teaching that they thought these children would find beneficial. This supports the evidence of the questionnaires, observations and interviews, from which the effective teachers appeared to use a wider range of diagnostic assessment strategies, to keep careful records and to be more likely to plan sessions carefully tailored to the needs of their children. A picture of most of the effective teachers as more diagnostic in their use of children's performance and more concerned with the children's learning emerges from this data.

The effective teachers' abilities to examine the reading and writing passages, and to make connections between the language levels involved, may be an indicator of how they know about language. They clearly did have an in-depth knowledge of the text, sentence and word levels of language but were much more likely to represent this knowledge in terms of what children could do. They were generally less able to show knowledge about language in the abstract sense of recognising particular forms such as phonemes or morphemes. Content knowledge for these teachers appeared to be highly embedded in their teaching of this knowledge.

The content of literacy lessons

In terms of content, the effective teachers' lessons that we observed showed a number of consistent features that strongly suggest an underpinning content knowledge. These teachers were focused in their aims for the lessons observed. Although the teachers' plans were not examined in detail, all were able to identify the focus and aims of a lesson to the interviewers, and this coincided with observers' accounts of that lesson. This was not always the case for the validation sample teachers. In addition, the effective teachers tended to identify the literacy focus of the lesson *to* the class of children, usually more than once during a lesson. The way they did this was often by discussion with the class about *why* a particular piece of literacy knowledge, or a particular reading or writing skill, was useful. This sort of discussion was much less common in the lessons of the validation group.

A brief example of this feature is the way Mrs J began her introduction to the class:

> Right, today, we are going to look at one of the features of *The Demon Headmaster* which you might not have noticed. That's the dialogue. What is dialogue. Can someone find some in the book? [writes the word 'dialogue' on the board and takes answers and examples from three children].
>
> The characters speaking to each other. It's one of the things that makes a character interesting and it is really important that we, the readers, understand exactly what the characters do say to each other. So we are going to see how that speech is set out in the book, so that the readers know who is speaking and how they are speaking.

After discussing the details of the conventions of dialogue, Mrs J again reinforced this point in introducing the task to the children:

> I want you to be able write out dialogue so that you can make your characters this interesting. You need to use this way of setting out speech to do this, so I am getting you all to write a dialogue today to practise these points. I want you to write a dialogue between two characters from the book, setting it out so that a reader can easily see

who is speaking. What are you going to use to set this out? [writes down the words 'capitals', 'commas', 'inverted commas' and 'new lines' on the board as the children call them out].

At the end of the session, Mrs J went over the main points of setting out direct speech and concluded with the words:

> OK, now we've practised setting out dialogue with characters you know from the book, we'll have to go on and write some for the characters we make up. And I want you to remember how to set out the speech so that you can write clear, interesting dialogue. So that a reader can understand easily. Good dialogue that's easy to read brings a character alive. It's vital to a good plot – one of you could be the next Gillian Cross.

Not only was Mrs J teaching her class about a specific punctuation rule but she was also signalling to them why it was important and what purpose it served. She was helping them to make a connection between word-level and text-level knowledge, and her teaching clearly drew upon her own knowledge of the features she was teaching.

The literacy focus of a lesson was not only discussed with the children but was also usually set in a context of a whole text or learning aim for the children. Key Stage 1 children, for instance, were repeatedly asked to suggest their own examples of the use of particular letter sounds. At Key Stage 2, teachers were more likely to use particular audiences or purposes for types of writing as the context of a literacy aim such as using adjectives or comprehension strategies. In both situations, teachers emphasised the function of literacy and the connections with ongoing, completed or future literacy activities. The effective teachers did not simply present a literacy point without context, whereas this happened repeatedly in the lessons of validation teachers. A lesson about setting out dialogue by one of the validation teachers, for instance, included reference to 'the rules for setting out direct speech' and negotiated these rules with the children. However, no mention was made of why direct speech was set out like this. This was in strong contrast to the attention given to function seen in the extract from Mrs J's lesson above.

The difference here between these two groups of teachers suggests a difference in their content knowledge in literacy, but not necessarily a difference in the extent of this knowledge. Rather, the distinction lies in the ways this knowledge was represented. The effective teachers appeared more able to see connections between the content they knew about, particularly between content at the textual and sentence/word levels. They were thus able to set items of sentence/word-level content into a whole text context and to ensure that these connections were made apparent to their pupils. This knowledge enabled them to be less dependent on published materials in their teaching and to work with pupils' own understanding, confident in the knowledge that they would be able to relate this readily to the goals for a particular lesson.

These connections tended not to be made by the validation teachers, which suggests that their knowledge was internally represented as discrete items of content. Because of this discreteness, they had much less scope for demonstrating at a deeper level the workings of the English language, lacking the knowledge to see opportunities for pointing out examples as they occurred in their own or their pupils' language use.

Of some relevance to the issue of content focus are the teachers' reasons for choosing to teach particular literacy content at a particular time. When we asked the teachers why they had chosen to cover content in a particular lesson, the categories of answers received included:

1 because it was planned (in which case we probed further);
2 because of identified children's literacy needs in developmental terms;
3 because of a progression in terms of planning literacy content;
4 because of a topic link.

The effective teachers generally described reasons for choosing particular content in greater detail than the validation teachers. This may reflect greater expertise in the subject and also a greater depth of content knowledge.

The effective teachers used reasons 2 and 3 consistently. Where they mentioned planning or their scheme of work as the reason for choosing the lesson content, we asked why it was like that and they gave us answers that were similar to categories 2 and 3. Many of the effective teachers gave detailed accounts of what particular children could do and what the next step in their learning was felt to be. They seemed to have a clear idea of the developmental sequences involved in learning the aspects of literacy discussed.

> Well, that's what they need to do in their writing now. They've seen me writing for them and they have done short items of composing. We have done oral stories and they have heard plenty of stories. I know they can use the sounds to get a good number of words. So its time for a little more challenging task. Pulling it all together in a story for someone else. I mean, I'm confident they can do it because I have reviewed the skills they need. It's just the job they need now. They will be really pleased with it too when its finished. Don't underestimate that sense of achievement. It really helps them learn.

> 'Well I know they're ready for that, those children.'
> 'How do you know?'
> 'I mean I know what they've done of course and how they did it. I know

what sounds they know and who has got concepts like "words" and so on. I test them regularly on sight vocabulary. I know what words they know. If you noticed the three who have sentence makers, they have 25–30 words they know by sight in the sentence makers. The others know 6–9 words by sight.'

The effective teachers also told us that they had selected items of content in terms of their place in a sequence of content.

Well, it's because of the preliminary work I've done. I have been building this up. I've shown them how to do word webs, how to do a brainstorm, but everything in the past has been quite teacher-directed and teacher-led. Now I feel they are able to take on more responsibility for their own work, so this task gets them to do that.

We're doing a study on poems. We're looking at different poems, looking at the way poems are structured, looking at the different devices poets use. The last session was on writing of poems and the structure. We talked about how poems are structured and how they are different from narrative writing. This follows on from that and leads on to later poems work.

We are learning about sounds and words as they are getting on to writing more themselves. So we have done initial sounds and initial two sounds, which most of them can cope with. There's a small group who aren't ready for this so I am doing ending sounds. We've done -og words – we did that last week and the week before and we're on to -at words. I introduced those this morning on the sheet on the easel, all the words ending in -at they could come up with and now we're putting them into sentences to see what you can do with these words.

Where the effective teachers referred to the place of the content in terms of the school, county or published scheme of work, they used either the needs of the children or the progression of literacy content as justification of this structure.

Well as part of our scheme of work we have a story writing focus for our term for this Y6. We've identified the different aspects of story writing we want to teach and we have got a planning sheet where we have mapped out what we want the very able, less able and capable to learn. It seemed a good time in the story to do this because we have been reading the book for a couple of weeks, they are thoroughly enjoying it and it came to an obvious point for them to do some of their own work on this. So it brings together the things they have been doing in the last four or five weeks.

The validation teachers explained their choice of content much more briefly than the effective teachers of literacy. They used all the reasons mentioned above but were much more likely to use categories 1 and 4. They generally chose content to fit in with the scheme of work or planning and, when asked, did not explain why the work was planned in this way. They pointed out that the English co-ordinator, year team or colleague had made these decisions either with or without their participation, but they did not say why. Three of the teachers said that they chose work to reflect the topic link, which was not a literacy theme, so that the work was chosen for a non-literacy reason. Two validation teachers also said that they had chosen this content as preparation for SATs. The very different use of reasons for choice reflects the balance of expertise of these teachers. They were co-ordinators of mathematics in their schools and appeared much less able to discuss children's needs or literacy progression than the effective teachers of literacy.

Reference to a developmental sequence in children's learning of literacy suggests a fairly secure knowledge of what children are learning. The fact that the effective teachers of literacy were able to do this consistently again implies an extensive knowledge base in literacy. Again, however, it was evident that the content knowledge that these teachers referred to was always firmly embedded in their analysis of what their children could do and should now be doing.

Linguistic terminology

During the classroom observations, we highlighted the ways teachers discussed literacy with their children and made careful note of the linguistic terminology used in presenting literacy lessons. The variety of terminology used was clearly circumscribed and included the following terms:

- **Word level**: alphabet, alphabetical order, rhyme, definition, beginning sound, middle sound, end sound, vowel, word, letter, sound, blend, magic *e*, homophone, synonym, digraph, prefix, spelling string.
- **Sentence level**: capital letter, full stop, sentence, speech mark, inverted comma, noun, thing word, adjective, describing word, contraction, apostrophe, word order, dialogue, conversation, apostrophe, question mark.
- **Text level**: predict, picture, caption, label, paragraph, planning, drafting, revising (plan, draft, revision), story, instructions, report, headings, ending, opening, character, setting, alliteration, ingredients, list, fiction, non-fiction, layout, address, salutation, skimming, scanning, highlight, key word, meaning, expression, image, simile.
- **Range of text types**: poem, author, illustrator, paperback and hardback, nursery rhyme, cover, ISBN, picture, script, play, recipe, dictionary, appreciate, comparison.

Although the effective teachers did not appear to use a wider variety of terms about language than the validation sample in an individual lesson, they did use them differently. The effective teachers not only defined terms that they used but offered more examples of each item. They often collected examples and discussed the function of the word before offering a definition. They chose a variety of examples that illustrated the definition rather than repeating formulaic definitions (such as 'a verb is a doing word') and asked children to supply examples of their own. The effective teachers were also observed to ask the children to explain terms to them at a number of points in the session, whereas the teachers in the validation sample did not do this in most cases. It appeared that the effective teachers had a greater depth of knowledge than the validation teachers and were able to use a variety of representations of particular ideas.

In addition to using standard linguistic terminology, the effective teachers were observed to pick out and discuss elements of language, eliciting functional definitions of word types, parts of words or sentence organisation without using a standard linguistic definition. For instance, a teacher introducing the idea of descriptive writing as part of a narrative opening drew up a list of the nouns and adjectives in the example passage. These were sorted by the children in terms of their function, without using the label 'noun' or 'adjective'.

An interpretation of teachers' subject knowledge in literacy

In this chapter, we have presented details about our findings about teachers' content knowledge in literacy. We have been concerned to point out the complexity of this issue. As far as we know, this was the first research study to attempt such an exploration of literacy subject knowledge and, perhaps unsurprisingly, our findings do not altogether support the hypotheses we originally generated in this area. In particular, we failed to find any real separation in effective teachers between content knowledge and pedagogical content knowledge in literacy. It seems to us that the effective teachers of literacy 'knew' their subject in quite a special way, which itself has many implications for initial training and continuing professional development.

The main findings of our research into teachers' subject knowledge of literacy suggest several important conclusions:

- All the teachers we worked with could recognise the different literacy teaching needs of Key Stage 1 and Key Stage 2 children.
- There were differences between the validation teachers and the effective teachers in their specifications of what children needed to know about reading and writing. While the effective teachers taught the codes of language (phonics, spelling, grammar, etc.) just as much as their validation colleagues, in general they placed more emphasis on children's recognition of the purposes and functions of reading and writing and

on the codes as tools to enable these processes. The validation teachers were more likely to emphasise technical knowledge about the codes of literacy than their purpose and to stress the importance of technical knowledge for its own sake rather than an ability to use it accurately and effectively.

- All the teachers had limited success at recognising some types of word in a sentence and some sub-word units out of context. The effective teachers were more likely to be able to pick out word types such as adjectives, adverbs, etc. but less able to identify such units as phonemes, onsets and rimes, and morphemes. Using more everyday terminology for these units still did not ensure total success for the teachers in recognising them. This casts doubt on the effective teachers' abstract knowledge of linguistic concepts such as phoneme.

- Despite this apparent lack of knowledge, these teachers were observed to use some of it in their teaching, particularly that connected with phonics. Our interpretation of this contradiction is that the effective teachers knew the material they were teaching in a particular way. It did not seem to be the case that they knew a body of knowledge (content) and then selected appropriate ways to represent it to their children (pedagogy). Rather, they appeared to know the material in the way they taught it to the children, which was usually as material that helped these children to read and write. The knowledge base of these teachers thus *was* their pedagogical content knowledge. This is rather a different concept of pedagogical content knowledge from that of Shulman (1987), as described earlier, for whom this refers to knowledge of ways of transforming content in order to represent it for others. Our interpretation of what we observed is that the effective teachers did not transform their knowledge in this way. In fact, at the time we studied them, they appeared only to know their material by how they represented it for their children. They may once have known this material differently, but, through experience of teaching it, their knowledge seemed to have become totally embedded in their pedagogical practices.

- When examining and judging samples of children's reading and writing, all the teachers were able to generate criteria and analyse mistakes, but the ways the two groups approached the task was different. The effective teachers were more highly diagnostic in the ways they approached the task and were more obviously able to generate sustainable explanations as to why children read or wrote as they did. In examining the pieces of writing, although the two groups mentioned similar features eventually, the effective teachers were quicker to focus on possible underlying causes of a child's writing behaviour. The validation sample required lots of prompting and time to reach an equivalent point. It is likely that, in a busy classroom context, they would not routinely make the same level of judgements made by the effective teachers. This suggests a further aspect of subject knowledge in which the effective teachers of literacy performed better: the knowledge of children and the ways they exhibit skills or skill problems in literacy.

- We also found evidence from observations of a limited range of linguistic terminology being used by teachers. It appeared that the way the two groups of teachers used linguistic terminology was different. The validation teachers were likely to teach definitions of the terms they used, whereas the effective teachers tended to begin with language functions and use these within a clear text setting before deriving a definition, which might well be arrived at in discussion with the children. Children in the classes of these teachers, while acquiring the necessary knowledge, were much more heavily involved in problem solving and theorising about language for themselves rather than being given only 'facts' to learn.

5 Teachers' beliefs about literacy teaching

Introduction

As we have already suggested, studies of teacher beliefs (e.g. Munby, 1984; Nespor, 1987; Richardson, 1994) suggest that the extent to which teachers adopt new instructional practices in their classrooms relates closely to the degree of alignment between their personal beliefs and the assumptions underlying particular teaching approaches. This suggests that, in order to understand teachers' classroom practices and to design professional development programmes that seek to change these, an understanding of teachers' beliefs is important. Nevertheless, the existing literature on teaching is weak in terms of evidence about the ways beliefs link to practice, especially in the teaching of literacy. We deliberately set out to investigate this link, and our working hypothesis was that the effective teachers of literacy would have developed a coherent set of beliefs about the nature and the learning of literacy that played a guiding role in their selection of teaching approaches. Thus our line of enquiry focused on the consistency between teachers' beliefs about literacy teaching, the teaching activities they said they valued and those activities that they actually used.

Our findings, in summary, indicate that, in reporting their views about the teaching of reading and writing, the effective teachers of literacy were much more likely than teachers in the validation sample to place a high priority on purpose, communication and composition. They also emphasised the importance of connecting word-level, sentence-level and text-level aspects of reading and writing in this construction. The effective teachers generally identified teaching activities that were consistent with their stated beliefs about the teaching of literacy. From our observations of the ways they translated their beliefs into classroom practice, it was clear that these teachers also made explicit to their pupils the connections between word-, sentence- and text-level aspects.

We used two main approaches to investigate teachers' beliefs about the teaching of literacy. First, as part of the questionnaire administered to both the effective teacher sample and the validation sample, teachers were asked to complete an orientation profile to determine their reported beliefs.

We also observed the practice of a number of teachers in both samples and interviewed them about this practice. Our aim was thus to check reported beliefs against the reality of classroom action to give a more valid account of the beliefs of these teachers.

Orientations towards the teaching of literacy

Our hypothesis was that the more effective teachers would have more fully developed practical theories about teaching literacy, which would govern their actions in classrooms at a strategic level. Such practical theories or beliefs are difficult to research, because they operate implicitly and create tendencies to act in certain ways rather than direct certainties about specific actions.

We found the concept of orientation useful as a way of thinking about teachers' beliefs or theories. It helped us to consider both the different degrees to which teachers were drawn to specific ideas and the extent to which such patterns of belief or theory were consistent both internally and with teachers' statements about their teaching strategies and their work in classrooms.

We used and adapted a model of orientation developed originally by Deford (1985) to try to identify the major patterns in orientation towards literacy teaching. Deford's model provides a series of attitude statements, which can be used to analyse the relative emphasis that teachers give to different beliefs about teaching reading. In adapting Deford's model, we:

- reduced the number of statements used in the instrument;
- rewrote them to be less American in tone;
- added a parallel set of statements about teaching strategies and about writing.

The broad patterns of orientation we worked with we refer to as:

For reading:
- a phonic orientation;
- a word orientation;
- a meaning or communication orientation.

For writing:
- a presentation orientation;
- a process orientation;
- a forms/purpose orientation.

There was no expectation that these orientations would be mutually exclusive.

In using the orientations in the questionnaire, we hoped to be able to discern:

- distinctive broad patterns of emphasis between groups of teachers;
- the extent to which teachers' statements about teaching strategies were consistent with their reported beliefs;
- the extent to which teachers demonstrated coherent patterns in their stated beliefs;
- the extent to which teachers' stated beliefs were consistent with what they actually did in classrooms.

In describing our findings, we need to describe the building blocks of our analysis step by step, but the significance of each element is only clear when the whole picture is assembled. It is therefore crucial not to take individual elements out of context. For example, although the teachers whose pupils made good learning gains, the effective teachers, did not express a strong orientation towards phonics, emphasising instead the importance of communicating and composing meaning, they did in fact teach phonics systematically. Their orientation towards communication led them to approach phonics as an important means to an end rather than as an end in itself.

Responses to attitude statements

The questionnaire distributed to all teachers in the research study contained twelve attitude statements, two representing each of the orientations to literacy described above. Teachers were asked to respond to these statements on the familiar strongly agree/agree/not sure/disagree/strongly disagree basis. Their responses were scored from 1 (strongly agree) to 5 (strongly disagree). The mean responses to each of the attitude statements is given in Table 5.1. Statements designed to reflect similar theoretical orientations have been grouped together, and the first column of the table gives details of these orientations. Mean responses that are less than 3 represent a tendency to agreement with the statement and those of more than 3, disagreement.

Results are given separately for each of the two groups, and the statistical differences between the two groups are indicated if these were at the 5 per cent level of confidence or less. (Statistical significances were calculated using the t statistic.) The results suggest that some significant differences in the beliefs about literacy were held by these two groups of teachers. These can be summarised as:

- The effective teachers of literacy tended to have an open stance towards a phonics theoretical orientation while the validation teachers were more drawn to it.

Table 5.1 Mean responses of both samples to attitude statements about literacy

Theoretical orientation	Attitude statements	Mean response of effective teachers	Mean response of validation teachers	Sig. diff.
A 'phonic' orientation	When children do not know a word, they should be instructed to sound out its parts.	2.66	2.01	**
	Phonic analysis (that is, breaking down a word into its sounds) is the most important form of analysis used when meeting new words.	3.24	2.49	**
A 'whole word' orientation	It is necessary to introduce new words before they appear in a child's reading book.	3.66	3.44	
	It is important for a word to be repeated a number of times after it has been introduced to ensure that it will become part of a child's sight vocabulary.	1.82	1.46	**
A 'meaning-centred' orientation	When coming to a word that is unknown, the reader should be encouraged to guess a meaning and carry on.	2.03	2.44	**
	If a child says 'house' for the written word 'home', the response should be left uncorrected.	2.46	2.9	*
A 'presentation' orientation	It is important to correct children's spellings as they write.	3.45	3.1	*
	Fluent, accurate handwriting is a very high priority in early writing teaching.	3.92	3.17	**
A 'process' orientation	If children have spelt a word wrongly but their attempt is clearly logically based it should usually be left uncorrected.	2.62	2.83	
	In the early stages, getting children to be confident in writing is a higher priority than making sure they are accurate.	1.38	1.39	
A 'forms' orientation	Most children's writing should be for audiences other than the teacher.	2.11	2.13	
	Young writers should choose their own reasons for writing.	2.56	2.57	

Key: * $= p < 0.5$ ** $= p < 0.1$

- Although both groups tended to disagree that young readers should be introduced to new words before meeting them in context in a book, the validation teachers were more likely to agree that repetition of words was important in early reading.
- The effective teachers were more likely to take a meaning-centred orientation to the teaching of reading than the validation teachers.
- The effective teachers of literacy generally disagreed with the prioritisation of presentation in the teaching of writing. The validation teachers tended to be neutral about this.

These differences were much more pronounced in beliefs about the teaching of reading, but it seems that, in general, the effective teachers felt more strongly that literacy teaching should prioritise meaning. Whether this translated into their attitudes towards literacy-teaching strategies and their use of teaching approaches is something we shall discuss later. We will also be exploring through classroom observation and interview how teachers incorporated the teaching of features of literacy such as phonic knowledge and spelling skills into an approach that prioritised meaning.

As a first step in investigating the issue of coherence in both groups' beliefs about literacy, correlations between the pairs of statements representing particular orientations were calculated. These are given for each group in Table 5.2. With the exception of the process orientation, these correlations were highly statistically significant in the effective teachers of literacy. That is, teachers who agreed with one of each pair of statements also tended to agree with the other. This level of agreement was slightly less in the validation teachers. The figures thus confirm our hypothesis so far: the effective teachers of literacy did seem to have more coherent beliefs about the teaching of literacy. The next step was to investigate whether

Table 5.2 Correlations between responses to attitude statements about literacy

Theoretical orientation	Correlation between the pairs of statements representing each orientation			
	Effective teachers	*Sig.*	*Validation teachers*	*Sig.*
A 'phonic' orientation	0.52	**	0.49	**
A 'whole word' orientation	0.30	**	0.27	*
A 'meaning-centred' orientation	0.35	**	0.16	
A 'presentation' orientation	0.31	**	0.35	**
A 'process' orientation	0.13		0.13	
A 'forms' orientation	0.41	**	0.33	**

Key: $* = p < 0.5$ $** = p < 0.1$

this coherence was apparent in their attitudes towards literacy-teaching activities.

Responses to suggested literacy teaching strategies

The questionnaire contained a list of twelve suggested literacy-teaching activities, selected to represent what we thought would be logical activities to choose if one held particular beliefs about the teaching of literacy. Two activities represented each of the six orientations to literacy described above. For each activity, teachers were asked to tick a box that best represented their view about whether the activity was useful in teaching reading and/or writing. The tick boxes were ordered as strongly agree/agree/not sure/disagree/strongly disagree, and their responses were scored from 1 (strongly agree) to 5 (strongly disagree).

The mean responses of each group to each of the teaching activities is given in Table 5.3. Activities felt to reflect similar theoretical orientations have been grouped together, and the first column of the table gives details of these orientations. Mean responses that are less than 3 represent positive feelings about the activity and those of more than 3, negative. Results are given separately for each of the two groups, and the statistical differences between the two groups are indicated if these were at the 5 per cent level of confidence or less. (Statistical significances were calculated using the *t* statistic.)

There were some significant differences in the reactions to these teaching activities of the effective teachers of literacy and of the validation sample teachers. These can be summarised as follows:

- The effective teachers were more positive than the validation teachers towards meaning-focused activities in the teaching of reading, rating more highly the activities of children listening to tape-recorded versions of stories while following the text in a book and the use of big books to model and share reading.
- They were less positive about what might be considered more 'traditional' approaches to teaching reading, such as children completing phonic worksheets and exercises, and the use of flashcards to teach children to read words by sight. These activities tend to be less contextualised than others in the list, and thus the feelings of the effective teachers towards them were consistent with their general preference for contextualised teaching of literacy.
- In terms of the teaching of writing, the effective teachers were less positive than the validation teachers about the use of spelling tests but more positive about asking children to comment upon and help to revise each other's writing.

Table 5.3 Mean responses of both samples to suggested literacy-teaching activities

Theoretical orientation	Teaching activities	Mean response of effective teachers	Mean response of validation teachers	Sig. diff.
A 'phonic' orientation	Teaching letter sounds as a way of helping children to build up words.	1.64	1.61	
	Children completing phonic worksheets and exercises.	3.04	2.51	**
A 'whole word' orientation	Using flashcards to teach children to read words by sight.	2.71	2.31	**
	Using graded reading schemes to structure children's introduction to reading.	2.42	2.11	*
A 'meaning-centred' orientation	Children listening to tape-recorded versions of stories while following the text in a book.	1.64	1.83	*
	Using big books with a group of children to model and share reading.	1.31	1.73	**
A 'presentation' orientation	Children copying or tracing over an adult's writing.	2.98	2.71	
	Regular spelling tests using published spelling lists.	3.40	2.75	**
A 'process' orientation	Children using the 'magic line' when writing: that is, when they reach a word they cannot spell, writing its initial sound followed by a line and then checking the correct spelling afterwards.	2.05	2.19	
	Asking children to comment upon and help to revise each other's writing.	1.55	1.93	**
A 'forms' orientation	Getting children to write to other children in other schools or areas of the country.	1.96	1.94	
	Using worksheets or frames to guide children's writing in particular forms.	2.29	2.39	

Key: * = $p < 0.5$ ** = $p < 0.1$

Table 5.4 Correlations between responses to literacy-teaching activities

Theoretical orientation	Correlation between responses to teaching activities representing each orientation			
	Effective teachers	*Sig.*	*Validation teachers*	*Sig.*
A 'phonic' orientation	0.27	**	0.45	**
A 'whole word' orientation	0.50	**	0.51	**
A 'meaning-centred' orientation	0.35	**	0.37	**
A 'presentation' orientation	0.33	**	0.09	
A 'process' orientation	0.25	**	0.24	
A 'forms' orientation	0.03		0.03	

Key: $* = p < 0.5$ $** = p < 0.1$

The differences between the two groups were much more pronounced in their feelings about reading activities than about writing activities, but, in general, it seems that the effective teachers responded more positively to literacy-teaching activities in which composition and communication were prime goals rather than those in which sounds and words were stressed for their own sakes.

As with the earlier attitude statements, correlations were also calculated between responses to pairs of activities representing particular approaches to literacy teaching. These are given for each group in Table 5.4. These correlations suggest that all the teachers completing the questionnaire were fairly consistent in their responses to the pairs of teaching activities chosen to represent each orientation to teaching reading.

Responses to the writing-teaching activities, however, showed a different picture. The effective teachers of literacy were consistent in responses to the pairs of teaching activities chosen to represent the presentation and the process orientation, whereas the validation group's responses to these pairs showed little relationship.

Coherence in beliefs about literacy teaching

One of our hypotheses was that the effective teachers of literacy would show a greater coherence in their belief systems about literacy. Accordingly, we needed to explore the relationship between the theoretical orientations to literacy teaching held by the two groups and their feelings about teaching activities that matched these orientations. We felt that coherent belief systems would be indicated through strength of agreement between theoretical orientations and attitudes to activities. To investigate this, we computed correlations between responses to each individual attitude statement and

Table 5.5 Responses to attitude statements and teaching activities showing significant correlation (effective teachers)

Pair of statements	Correlation	Sig.
Phonic orientation statement 1 and phonic teaching activity 1	0.28	**
Phonic orientation statement 1 and phonic teaching activity 2	0.34	**
Phonic orientation statement 2 and phonic teaching activity 1	0.31	**
Phonic orientation statement 2 and phonic teaching activity 2	0.25	**
Whole-word orientation statement 1 and whole-word teaching activity 1	0.31	**
Whole-word orientation statement 1 and whole-word teaching activity 2	0.19	**
Whole-word orientation statement 2 and whole-word teaching activity 1	0.33	**
Whole-word orientation statement 2 and whole-word teaching activity 2	0.43	**
Meaning-centred orientation statement 1 and meaning-centred teaching activity 2	0.27	**
Meaning-centred orientation statement 2 and meaning-centred teaching activity 1	0.23	**
Meaning-centred orientation statement 2 and meaning-centred teaching activity 2	0.21	**
Process orientation statement 2 and process teaching activity 2	0.21	**
Presentation orientation statement 1 and presentation teaching activity 1	0.24	**
Presentation orientation statement 1 and presentation teaching activity 2	0.21	**
Presentation orientation statement 2 and presentation teaching activity 2	0.32	**
Forms orientation statement 1 and forms teaching activity 1	0.22	**
Forms orientation statement 2 and forms teaching activity 1	0.20	**

Key: $* = p < 0.5$ $** = p < 0.1$

feelings about each of the two teaching activities we judged would fit with that orientation. Table 5.5 shows the statistically significant correlations between pairs of statements of the effective teachers of literacy. Of the twenty-four possible comparisons in this analysis, these teachers showed very significant levels of agreement in seventeen, suggesting a very high level of coherence between their attitudes towards literacy and their feelings about particular teaching activities.

The levels of agreement in the responses of the validation teachers were much less likely to be significant. Table 5.6 shows that, for this sample, statistically significant correlations were found for only seven pairs of statements.

The results shown in the last two tables together support our hypothesis. The effective teachers of literacy were more likely to show coherence between their beliefs about the learning of literacy and about approaches to its teaching. This match between beliefs about literacy and attitudes towards teaching approaches suggests that these teachers had belief systems about literacy that influenced their selection of approaches to teaching. We need to be cautious about this, however. Although these results demonstrate that what the effective teachers of literacy appeared to believe about literacy matched what they *said* they felt about particular kinds of teaching activity, it is also important to consider how this related to what these teachers actually did in their classrooms.

Table 5.6 Responses to attitude statements and teaching activities showing significant correlation (validation teachers)

Pair of statements	Correlation	Sig.
Phonic orientation statement 2 and phonic teaching activity 1	0.26	*
Whole-word orientation statement 1 and whole-word teaching activity 1	0.49	**
Whole-word orientation statement 1 and whole-word teaching activity 2	0.35	**
Whole-word orientation statement 2 and whole-word teaching activity 1	0.37	**
Whole-word orientation statement 2 and whole-word teaching activity 2	0.35	**
Presentation orientation statement 1 and presentation teaching activity 1	0.36	**
Presentation orientation statement 1 and presentation teaching activity 2	0.33	**

Key: $* = p < 0.5$ $** = p < 0.1$

Beliefs and action

Two sub-samples of teachers, as explained elsewhere, were twice observed teaching literacy and were subsequently interviewed about this teaching. The teachers observed were asked to teach 'a normal literacy session', and the strategies, techniques and content of the lessons seen reflected the full range of activities suggested by the questionnaire results.

A number of issues about teacher's beliefs about literacy and its teaching were identified from the questionnaire data for further exploration during the lesson observations and interviews:

- How did the effective teachers' strong orientation towards meaning-centred statements about literacy teaching at the level of beliefs translate into classroom practice?
- How did the effective teachers of literacy marry the emphasis they placed on breaking down words as an important teaching strategy with their beliefs about phonics and the importance of focusing explicitly upon meaning?
- How did the effective teachers teach letter sounds, given their disinclination to use phonic worksheets?
- Given the effective teachers' emphasis upon confidence in writing in the early stages, how did they try to ensure well-presented and accurate writing?
- Was there any coherence between what the teachers reported themselves as doing in the questionnaires and what they actually did in practice? The gap between self-report and action is a very familiar phenomenon noted in a number of social science research areas.

We will report our findings regarding these questions under several headings.

Making connections: levels of language study

The observed teaching of the effective teachers of literacy reflected their reported beliefs in the importance of communication and composition. They were also quite clearly systematically teaching elements of language such as sentence features and the ways words were constructed, for example phonologically. The ways in which they brought together these levels of language study were significant and rather different to the approaches generally used by the validation teachers.

A noticeable feature of the teaching of the effective teachers was the very wide range of texts used in their sessions. These were chosen by the teachers to be suitable for the literacy purposes of their lessons. They included class novels, stories that illustrated particular narrative features and conventions of writing, information books with particular book conventions, and good-quality literature matched to the children's levels of individual and group reading ability.

The effective teachers of literacy chose to teach features of language such as sound patterns and word functions in the context of larger units of texts and to emphasise the function of a particular element of language. In doing this, they explicitly made connections for their pupils between language elements at the text, sentence and word levels.

They also tended to set fewer published exercises than the teachers in the validation sample, although there was clear evidence that they did use exercises. There were, however, several distinctive features about the ways in which these were used. In particular, it seemed from our observations that the effective teachers of literacy always ensured that they gave pupils clear instructions about the use of the exercise. Teachers made it clear to pupils what the point of an exercise was, how they should tackle it and what they should expect to learn from it. This kind of clarity was not usually evident in the lessons of the validation teachers.

The issue of meaning was particularly important in relation to grammar and punctuation lessons. The effective teachers of literacy were much more likely to spend time discussing the use of a grammatical structure and defining it by illustrating its role in a sentence. They used grammar to *describe* language. The children in their classes were often asked to deduce grammatical rules from presented extracts of language, often taken from shared texts. The teacher contributed to ensure their ideas were sensible, but the children in lessons like this were very heavily involved in making sense of the language rules they were learning. The validation teachers, on the other hand, were much more likely to use grammar to *prescribe* rules for writing. Rules were presented to children as things they had to follow, but there was little attempt to get them to understand why. These practices seem to us to represent very different concepts of the nature and function of sentence grammar.

What was distinctive, therefore, about the effective teachers' work was the deliberate ways in which they linked work on sentences and/or words to whole texts. Language study for their pupils was embedded in experience of texts so the teachers could point out connections between language levels in ways that made it more likely that the pupils themselves would see these connections.

The teaching of phonics

From the questionnaire, it appeared that the effective teachers of literacy were less positive about a phonic orientation to teaching reading than were the validation sample, agreeing that breaking down words to sounds was a useful reading strategy but not that it was the most important strategy. We looked more closely at the practice of both groups in this area and found important differences in the ways in which each saw the purpose of phonics and taught this to their children.

Although the effective teachers did not say that phonics was their priority in teaching reading, there was plenty of evidence that they were teaching sound–symbol correspondences in a planned, systematic way. Of the twenty-six effective teachers' sessions observed in the second round of observations, ten had a planned phonics component. In all these cases the teachers, when asked about the content of the lesson, identified sound recognition as one of their teaching aims. This included the study of particular letter sounds, blends and digraphs by the whole class each week, although the classes were often organised so that different groups did the tasks at different times. This resulted in some classes discussing a particular sound several times in class introductions.

The phonics sessions we observed included whole class introductions where the teacher picked out the chosen sound from a sentence or text. The teachers wrote a sound on boards or flipcharts and collected words that featured that sound. They drew attention to the letters involved in the sounds, including letter names, position of these letters in the alphabet and letter formation. Teachers referred to other activities such as sound tables and television programmes, which they used to feature the sound and place it firmly in a classroom context. A great deal of emphasis was placed on when the sound in question would be encountered. Despite the questionnaire finding that effective teachers were less likely to use phonic worksheets, we observed five teachers setting worksheets as follow-up activities to a class discussion session. Some of these were related to the big books the teacher had been using. Three examples had been made by the teacher; the others came from major reading schemes. One teacher discussed this with us:

> I use the sheets, from another scheme, not ours actually, but they are better than the ones in ours. It's the way they use the stories. I use them as follow-up. A check. And to be honest, it does keep them busy while I work with the others.

Another six effective teacher lessons we observed had a sound identification component, including reference to initial sounds in big books read for other purposes, discussion of the sounds of words used in handwriting practice and references to sound rules in spellings used for writing. However, these were not mentioned by teachers as specific teaching aims.

In addition to sound and letter study, we observed four sessions that included activities with emphasis on rhymes. The teachers who taught these sessions reported rhyme recognition as one of their aims, and the sessions included the use of nursery rhymes and nonsense poems. All started with a whole class introduction, including repeating poems, rhymes and jingles in unison and picking out the rhymes. The teachers asked children to invent other rhymes and wrote up rhyming words to look at the letters used.

We observed three sessions that involved individual children reading with teachers and two where classroom assistants read with children. In all of these cases, the teachers were observed to point out or ask children to use initial sounds to help word attack, as well as using other prompts like questions about the story and asking the child to read past the word then come back to try to read it.

Although the effective teachers were addressing phonics systematically and made real efforts to plan and monitor it in their routine teaching of reading, they did not show an orientation towards phonics in their beliefs. It was apparently seen as a necessary, but not a sufficient, part of the teaching of reading: as a means to an end rather than as a goal in its own right.

During interviews, the teachers indicated that they had clear systems for teaching phonics, although these differed from school to school. Some linked the order of phonics teaching to handwriting, others to a progression of 'difficulty' of sounds or perceived developmental sequence, and still others to the pattern set by television programmes or schemes.

> We are learning about sounds and words as they are getting on to writing more themselves. So we have done initial sounds and initial two sounds, which most of them can cope with. There's a small group who aren't ready for these so I am doing ending sounds. We've done -og words – we did that last week and the week before and we're on to -at words. I introduced those this morning on the sheet on the easel, all the words ending in -at they could come up with and now we're putting them into sentences to see what you can do with these words.

> I've known since the start of term that lots of those children know those sounds, but I want to consolidate the concept of letter sound and use the sounds they know to go on to find other words with those sounds.

The lessons emphasised the role of sounds in reading and writing, and placed emphasis upon children's developing understanding of how the sound system of language could be used to offer access to stories, messages and other texts.

By contrast, the lessons of the validation teachers that we observed that had a phonic element tended to be managed quite differently. Phonics worksheets were heavily used, but little attempt was made to help children to apply the phonic blends they were learning to the reading of continuous texts. When questioned about their selection of the lesson content, these teachers were much more likely to reply that this was decided for them, usually citing a scheme of work agreed by the school as their rationale for a teaching order. We observed very little use of big books or nursery rhymes as a vehicle for introducing and discussing sounds.

The teaching of writing

The effective teachers also gave little emphasis to a presentation orientation towards writing. They strongly agreed that confidence in writing was more important than accuracy in the early stages of writing, and they did not agree with the validation teachers that the use of tests of published spelling lists was helpful. Again, close examination of how such beliefs are manifested in practice reveals a more complex picture.

Our observations suggest that the effective teachers were much more likely than the validation sample to prioritise other aspects of writing than presentation and more likely to separate the presentation aspects from composition in their teaching. However, they did do handwriting and spelling work at other times. The validation teachers were more likely to include both composition and presentation as teaching aims for a single session. This suggests rather more clarity of teaching aims in the effective teachers and less risk of these aims being confused by children trying to focus on too much at once.

Of the effective teachers' lessons observed, sixteen included writing tasks where the emphasis was placed on aspects of writing such as content (ideas), structure (of letters, stories, reports), text features such as paragraphs and chronological order, audience awareness (usually for letters), choice of words, planning, drafting and editing, alliteration, precis, rhyme, and images. The teachers were clear that these aspects of the sessions were the main teaching content and that this was what they wanted the children to learn. All these lessons did, nevertheless, contain some references to the presentation and spelling of writing. In some, the teachers pointed out that presentation and spelling were not important criteria in this particular lesson and would be dealt with later. However, the children did have a range of strategies for spelling words, and these were used as a matter of routine. Most of the teachers also emphasised at some point the use of sentences, capital letters and full stops.

We also observed ten sessions where one or more activities had a specific presentation or spelling focus that the teacher identified as a learning outcome for the session. These activities included structured handwriting practice, spelling rules practice (magic *e*, for instance, or dropping -e to add -ing) and copying out final drafts of writing for presentation purposes. We saw two spelling tests being given. One of these used words with a common visual spelling pattern, and the other was individual to each child, tested by another, of words spelled incorrectly the previous week. We did not see published spelling lists used in the classes of effective teachers.

Summary

In summarising the project's findings concerning teachers' beliefs about the teaching and learning of literacy, several points stand out as important:

- The effective teachers of literacy tended to place a high value upon communication and composition in their views about the teaching of reading and writing; that is, they believed that the creation of meaning in literacy was fundamental. They were more coherent in their belief systems about the teaching of literacy and tended to favour teaching activities that explicitly emphasised the deriving and the creating of meaning. In much of their teaching, they were at pains to stress to pupils the purposes and functions of reading and writing tasks.

- Although they emphasised purpose, communication and composition in their belief statements, this did not mean that the more technical aspects of reading and writing processes were neglected. There was plenty of evidence that such aspects as phonic knowledge, spelling, grammatical knowledge and punctuation were prominent in the teaching of effective teachers of literacy. However, technical aspects of literacy tended to be approached in quite different ways by the effective teachers than by most of the teachers in the validation sample, i.e. as means to an end rather than an end in themselves.

- The key difference in approach was in the effective teachers' emphasis on embedding systematic attention to word- and sentence-level aspects of reading and writing within whole-text activities that were both meaningful and explained clearly to pupils. Teachers in the validation sample were more likely to teach technical features as discrete skills for their own sakes, and they did not necessarily ensure that pupils understood the wider purpose of such skills in reading and writing.

- Our finding concerning the beliefs of this group of effective teachers of literacy, that they prioritised the creation of meaning in their literacy teaching, thus reflects not that they failed to emphasise such skills as phonics, spelling, grammar, etc. but rather that they were trying very hard to ensure that such skills were developed in children with a clear eye to the children's awareness of their importance and function.

6 Knowledge, beliefs and practice in effective teachers of literacy

Introduction

Central to the argument presented in this account of our research project is the assumption that an important factor in children's achievement in literacy is the teaching they experience in class. This is circumscribed by a variety of social, curricular and resource-based factors, but the teacher remains at the heart of the teaching process, selecting, structuring and presenting the content to be taught and so influencing directly the learning of literacy.

This research sought to examine whether effective teachers of literacy:

- systematically matched particular teaching methods, materials and classroom tasks to the needs of pupils;
- had a well-developed knowledge of the subject and its pedagogical principles, which underpinned their teaching;
- had coherent belief systems about the teaching of their subject.

Although previous research had not demonstrated that these features were characteristic of effective teachers of *literacy*, they gave us a research focus and a set of working hypotheses, as outlined earlier in this report.

The practices of literacy teachers

The literature on effective teaching in literacy suggests that there are particular teaching techniques that appear to be linked to pupil progress in reading and writing. Our evidence suggests that effective teachers of literacy were likely to employ such techniques in a strategic way; that is, with a very clear purpose linked to the identified literacy needs of specific pupils. The teaching techniques we specifically investigated included the following:

- the deliberate and systematic teaching of the formal structures of written language;

- the creation of 'literate environments' designed to enhance children's understandings of the functions of literacy and to provide opportunities for regular and sustained practice of literacy skills;
- the provision of a range of models and examples of effective use of reading and writing;
- the design and provision of focused tasks appropriate to pupils' ages and abilities with academic content that would engage their full attention and enthusiasm;
- the continuous monitoring of pupils' progress through the tasks provided and the use of assessment to inform teaching and report on progress;
- the assistance given to pupils in making explicit and systematic connections between text, sentence and word levels of language knowledge.

Our findings suggest that the ways in which teachers used particular practices reflected their beliefs about teaching and learning literacy. This was particularly evident in the ways the effective teachers tended to teach specific elements of language by emphasising their functions rather than by simply giving sets of rules. It was also evident in their concern to provide meaningful contexts for pupils' work in literacy.

Literacy teachers' knowledge

There was evidence that effective teachers of other subjects tended to possess a well-developed knowledge base in those subjects. However, it had not yet been established that effective teachers of literacy were in a similar position with regard to their 'subject'. For the purpose of this research, we extrapolated from research on teachers of other subjects and developed a series of detailed hypotheses pertaining to teachers of literacy. These were outlined in Chapter 1.

The study investigated these aspects of subject knowledge and found that the literacy content knowledge of effective teachers of literacy appeared to be embedded in their teaching; that is, it was understood and known in relation to a practical teaching context rather than in a formalised, abstract way. The effective teachers of literacy taught children elements of language in ways that emphasised getting them to understand how parts of language work, how levels of language knowledge are connected, and when and how these language features are used. This contrasted with the tendency among the validation teachers to teach language as a set of rules and definitions.

We suggest that the content knowledge held by effective teachers of literacy could not readily be separated from an understanding of its use or from their beliefs about how it should be taught. This has very particular implications for teacher education, which we will discuss later.

Literacy teachers' beliefs

Evidence from our research supports our hypothesis that effective teachers of literacy would have a coherent set of beliefs about the teaching and the learning of literacy, which would influence their selection of teaching approaches. The findings indicate that the effective teachers of literacy were likely to believe that reading and writing were principally concerned with the communication of meaning and that technical features of language were taught as a means to this end. They therefore placed high value upon composition, understanding of text, and the purposes and use of elements of language. They were less likely to stress language rules as formulae to be applied.

Effective teachers at work

At this point, we will describe in further detail two effective teachers of literacy from our sample. These two teachers embodied many of the findings of the research and in describing them in detail we can offer a flavour of the knowledge, beliefs and teaching practices of the effective teachers of literacy in the study. For each teacher, we will include an account of a single teaching session that we observed and a summary of their beliefs and knowledge taken from the data we collected during the project. We will conclude by summarising what it was about these two teachers that characterised them as effective teachers of literacy. It should be remembered that these teachers were studied before teaching approaches such as those embodied in the National Literacy Strategy and the literacy hour were current.

Effective teacher 1: Mrs W

Training and professional development

Mrs W had A levels in science subjects and qualified as a teacher with a Cert. Ed. in the late 1970s following three years of study. She had been teaching in primary schools for more than ten years, during which time she had taught both juniors and infants. Her current post included responsibility for English in a suburban first school with seven classes, where she had a class of Y2 children.

Mrs W felt that her initial teacher education took place too long ago to be relevant to her teaching now. In the current year, Mrs W had been involved in one–five days of in-service training focused on the teaching of reading and writing, which included sessions that she led in school and two short LEA courses at a local teachers' centre. She felt that the short courses had kept her in touch with recent initiatives but had not particularly affected her views about the teaching of literacy.

When asked what has been significant to her in becoming a teacher of literacy, Mrs W identified a number of experiences. One was the Certificate of Advanced Professional Studies (CAPS) in primary language, which she completed two years ago at the local university. She said that this course gave her time to consider the whole basis of her literacy teaching and to forge a strong philosophy about literacy teaching. This had guided her choice of teaching methods and materials and given her clear principles for using these. Certain tutors and course sessions, especially lectures, and working with other teachers to complete her own research had inspired and enthused Mrs W. Her literacy teaching philosophy had been particularly useful in assimilating new initiatives in recent years, especially in conjunction with the school-based work she had done to write a new scheme of work. This had given her the opportunity to spend time in the classes of her colleagues and talk with them. She felt that this had not only benefited the school by ensuring that the scheme of work was coherent, practical and 'owned' by the whole staff, but also that it had improved her classroom skills and given her new ideas.

Mrs W felt that her role as English co-ordinator was an important factor in her development as an effective teacher of literacy, as she felt it gave her professional responsibility and really 'got her into' literacy. Mrs W also identified the short courses she had attended and the co-ordinator's support group as important in 'keeping up to date' in the teaching of literacy, but she cautioned that she did not make changes to her approaches to teaching without considering them very carefully and discussing them with other teachers.

Mrs W found the content of her CAPS course relevant to her needs and generally found short courses interesting. In her questionnaire, she marked courses on grammar and phonological awareness as the least useful she had attended; she felt that these were much less practically relevant than the others she had enjoyed.

Literacy teaching practices

We observed Mrs W teach two sessions, one of which is reported below. In both sessions, Mrs W organised two activities and divided the class so that some children worked with ancillary staff or students. She showed us her planning for the sessions on school planning sheets that she had helped to develop. Mrs W was happy to show us her record book, in which she regularly made notes about children's performance in English, the children's individual reading records, which included detailed comments from teachers, helpers and parents, and the results from the standardised reading tests she administers twice a year. She could tell us, in detail, about the performance of individual pupils.

Mrs W's room included displays of topic and fiction books, labels on all equipment and posters telling children how to change library books.

The displays on the walls were at the children's eye level and contained questions about a poster as well as work by the children. A set of stories written as books and bound by the children was available for others to read. A listening centre, in the book area, was used by some of the children, who were browsing among the books, and a good range of taped stories was available.

In the lesson we observed, Mrs W started by doing a big book session with all the children in the class, which took about 20 minutes. The children clearly knew the routine and settled immediately. They were attentive and enthusiastic throughout both sessions. Mrs W started by asking children questions about the cover of the book, such as 'What do you think it will be about?' and 'How do you know?' and picked up their responses about the title, picture and author. She repeated these terms and added 'illustration' when she asked the children more about their ideas. When she turned the first page she pointed out the title and author again and asked the children what the ISBN meant. Several of them knew, but others obviously did not, so she explained.

Mrs W read the book in unison with the class, pausing before the final word of each line to see whether they could guess the rhyming word. Within a page or two, all the children were eagerly offering guesses. Mrs W also pointed out the beginning sound of ch-, th- and ph- words and -ing suffixes, which seemed to be a focus for some children. After the first reading, children were picked to read out a line each. Mrs W then went through and read out the rhymes.

Mrs W asked children questions about the story and what they thought about it, commenting on the funny bits and laughing with the children. Using the paper on the easel, she wrote up some words and asked the children for other words that rhymed with them. At first only a few children made guesses, but within four or five guesses the majority of the children seemed to have ideas to offer. Mrs W then picked out some words ending in -ing and collected more from the children in the same way, asking the children to come up and write them on the easel.

Following the big book session, Mrs W set the children working in three groups. One group went to browse among the books and read individually with an ancillary teacher. Another group went off to work on a comprehension passage related to the big book they had just read, with the support of a student. Mrs W said that all the children would complete these activities but at different times, so that the extra assistance of helpers and parents could be used effectively.

Mrs W herself worked with sixteen children on a cloze passage written on the blackboard. It was the start of a fairy story, as story beginnings were the writing focus for the fortnight in the class. The children were asked to read the passage carefully and given a few moments to do so. Individuals then volunteered to read it out sentence by sentence, saying 'something' for each blank. Mrs W pointed out the full stops and capitals around each sentence. Mrs W read the passage through aloud and then asked the children what it was about and how they knew. The children picked out the clues of standard phrases such as 'once upon a . . .' and items of meaning to suggest a theme and some detail for the story. They then worked in twos and threes to make a list of the words that would fit into the blanks. This took about 15 minutes. Mrs W then went through the passage, evaluating all answers and asking the children to evaluate them against the questions 'Does that make sense?' and 'Does it sound right like that?'. Mrs W also repeatedly asked children how they had worked out a word. One child said he had 'read over' the spaces to see what was needed, by which he meant reading the text with appropriate intonation and a slight pause at each gap. Mrs W asked others if they could do this. She then demonstrated how you could 'read over' a space to see what would make sense and sound right in the space.

Children were keen to defend their choice of words and say why alternatives did not make sense or sounded wrong. Mrs W tried out all the suggestions and accepted answers with appropriate meanings that were the right parts of speech, but she allowed several possible answers in some spaces, saying which ones she preferred and why. Finally, Mrs W read the whole passage with the spaces filled, reading out the alternatives, congratulated the children and reminded them that 'reading over' a space or word they didn't know was another way to help them to guess what would make sense and what would sound right.

When Mrs W was asked about this session, she identified the literacy content as 'a big book session, with rhymes and *-ing* as the focus'. She said that she had also emphasised three particular sounds as she was concerned about a small group of children who were still having difficulty with them. The second part of the session she called 'reading a story beginning to practise using semantic and syntactic reading cues'. She identified the children who could do rhymes and -ing words and use a full range of reading cues to some extent, and those who were still starting on these skills.

Beliefs about the teaching of literacy

The beliefs section of Mrs W's questionnaire suggested that she was moderately oriented towards a view of teaching reading that emphasised the communication of meaning as a vehicle through which to teach processes and towards an orientation in teaching writing that emphasised children composing. Her reactions to the tasks suggested in the questionnaire were consistent with these beliefs, and she strongly approved of the use of taped books, big books and teaching children to revise in writing. In her interview, she said that she had a very strong philosophy about teaching reading and writing, which was based on the need for children to understand how and why they should read and write. She aimed to make all tasks understandable and, for this reason, she preferred tasks involving whole texts like stories or posters through which she was able to teach features ranging from knowledge of how texts are constructed to detailed items about grammar, etc. Mrs W also pointed out that, while she liked children to share books and do 'emergent' writing, she had structured hand-writing, phonics and spelling schemes of work that recognised and built on children's achievements and made sure they were 'always moving on' and that she knew exactly what they could do.

Subject knowledge for teaching literacy

In her questionnaire, Mrs W wrote that children beginning to read should learn:

> that books are exciting, how a book works, and to talk like a book, using memory, initially, to help them make stories from books themselves.

In writing, children needed:

> a model from other children and adults, of writing, to write as part of play situations and to recognise when writing is useful.

At Key Stage 2, young readers needed:

> to be able to express critical opinions about books. To use books and other material to retrieve information and to enjoy a wider range of book types,

while young writers needed:

> to continue to develop different writing styles. To learn about the language of writing so that they can talk about it. To continue to progress in the technicalities of writing, including spelling, grammar, etc.

Mrs W had clear ideas about the differences between early literacy and literacy at Key Stage 2. She chose things that reflected her beliefs in enjoyment and creation of meaning, but also that reflected her concern to get children to understand how literacy works and what they should do. This was demonstrated practically in the way she used questioning and modelling in her teaching, such as in her use of shared reading involving a big book, during the course of reading which she systematically engaged children in discussion of textual features such as title, author and illustrations before moving on to work on beginning sounds in words.

   In the literacy quiz, Mrs W scored well above the average for effective teachers. She was able to recognise nouns, verbs, adjectives, adverbs, pronouns, prepositions and articles as well as syllables and morphemes. She could not manage phonemic or sound segmentation. This was rather surprising, as in the lesson observed she had broken down four words into sounds on the easel for the children and spent some time showing us her scheme of work for teaching sounds.

She scored 18 on the Children's Author Recognition Test (the same as the mean for effective teachers), suggesting that she had a good knowledge of children's literature. Mrs W was very analytical in her discussion of the quiz examples of pupils' writing and reading. She raised almost every possible point. In the writing samples, she mentioned the content and structural issues first, then discussed spelling and capitals. In the reading samples, she asked many questions about the children's related experience and gave a very thorough assessment, full of expert inference.

Effective teacher 2: Miss L

Training and professional development

Miss L had English, biology and French A levels as well as a BEd degree, which she had completed in 1992. She had been teaching for four years in a junior school of twelve classes, where she had been English co-ordinator for a year. For the past two years she had taught Y3. When asked what had helped her to become an effective teacher of literacy, Miss L replied:

> Well, I've brought things with me from college of course, and I've seen other people working and been into schools and seen different things happening there. Of course, I've had good courses and support.

Miss L found her initial teacher education useful in preparing her to teach and could pick out sessions and issues that had been particularly important for her, both in her university and on school practice.

> When I came here four years ago I didn't feel in any way under-prepared. I felt lucky, I mean it might have been a particularly good course, but I could tackle most things and you learn through experience. When things go wrong you think 'I won't do that again' and you do learn management skills with experience too.

Miss L felt that she had learned at least as much since she started teaching, especially about assessment.

Miss L had participated in five days of literacy in-service provision in the previous year. Three of these days were organised by her to bring the English adviser into school to work on school needs as identified in a pre-OFSTED inspection. The other two were days out in co-ordinators' workshops. In her experience of Continuing Professional Development (CPD), she found opportunities to try out ideas in the classroom, practical feedback from an expert and working with other teachers particularly useful. She also identified involvement in an LEA project to select suitable reading materials for each year group as particularly important. Miss L felt that becoming English co-ordinator had had most effect on her knowledge and practice, since, as a result, she had started to read publications, keep up to date with ideas and initiatives and make contact with other co-ordinators. When rating the content of literacy professional development sessions, Miss L found sessions on reading and writing processes most useful and sessions on grammar and spelling development least useful as she found these hard to recall.

Literacy teaching practices

Miss L taught more than one activity during both the sessions we observed. The session reported here was the first session we observed and involved both a reading carousel session and a whole class letter-writing activity. Miss L had very explicit termly, fortnightly and daily plans that showed us that this session was part of a scheme of work for letter writing. Miss L also showed us her records of pupils' progress, including standardised scores, observation notes, individual reading sheets and miscue analysis (in some cases). All the children had a portfolio of work, which they chose in conjunction with the teacher and parents to 'show what they could do'.

Miss L's room was visually stimulating, with colourful book cover displays, word webs about the current topic, charts of spelling strings, posters about editing text, book rating scales and other labels. The room contained a book corner with a range of good-quality (well-thumbed) fiction books and a smaller display of topic books from the library service. The children clearly displayed a proportion of the work themselves and did so to a high standard. Outside the class, in the library, there were displays of the Dewey system, of books and listening centres, taped books, and books on CD-ROM.

In the lesson we observed, Miss L started the afternoon with a reading carousel. This involved children consulting a chart on the wall and dividing into groups. Each group did one of the following tasks:

- reading and discussing a book with a parent who was sitting in the library;
- doing a listening task involving a taped book and a work card of questions;
- group reading from a set of the same books with another parent in the library;
- browsing in the book corner among non-fiction books;
- completing a dictionary-use task.

Miss L worked with the dictionary group. She explained that all the children would complete all these tasks each week, although next week she would choose a new task to replace the dictionary task. The children were engaged and enthusiastic. They talked quietly with each other and with the parents and teachers. After 20 minutes, the groups put away the activities and settled into their places. As the children packed up, Miss L took brief verbal reports from the two parents about the performance of individual children and the groups, and she looked at the notes the parents had made on the sheets she had provided for them. She later explained that she worked with these parents regularly and had trained them to monitor and record these tasks.

For the second part of the session, Miss L introduced a letter-writing task. She reminded the children that next year they would be Y4 and they discussed their expectations and new teacher. Miss L then said that they should all write to that teacher so that the new teacher could have some information about her class in advance. This was a normal transition task in the school, and all the children would do it. Miss L discussed with the children what they would like to tell the teacher about themselves, their personalities and their strengths at school. She asked them how they wanted their new teacher to think about them. She then chose several responses and discussed different ways in which they might express one idea to give different impressions. Finally, Miss L discussed how such a letter might be set out, including address, salutation and paragraphing. Using the notes accumulated on the whiteboard from the introduction, which included prompts for content and layout, Miss L wrote a sample letter on the flipchart to tell her next class what they might expect when they come up to her. The children made suggestions about content and layout.

Miss L then described the task to the children again, stressing that they were to write a first draft, which would need to be edited later. Miss L told the children that they had 30 minutes to do their drafts, and she informed the whole class when 15 minutes had elapsed and when there were only 5 minutes left. She asked the children to work in their seatwork groups and pointed out some sources of support. One group used the notes on the board as prompts. A second group used a poster about letter writing on the wall, which gave rather more detailed prompts. Miss L talked through the poster so that they were all aware of its contents and how to use it. For two groups she provided writing frames, which offered sentences to help children to organise paragraphs. Miss L worked with one of these groups and only occasionally went around the class to check on the progress of other pupils.

At the end of the session, most of the children had completed drafts. Miss L asked for volunteers to read out paragraphs. She selected four children, who read out their work and accepted comments from them about the content, the impression created and whether the piece was all on one theme, so being a paragraph. Miss L concluded the lesson by saying that they would revise and edit the pieces on Thursday.

Beliefs about the teaching of literacy

The beliefs section of Miss L's questionnaire suggested that she tended towards an orientation in the teaching of reading that stressed the importance of communication and an orientation in the teaching of writing that stressed the writing process. She disapproved, in particular, of an emphasis on writing presentation that overwhelmed composition. The tasks in the questionnaire that she valued were consistent with these views: she selected big books, taped stories, writing frames and revising writing over other tasks. At interview, Miss L talked about the need for children to enjoy reading, develop confidence and receive enough support. She seemed particularly concerned with rigorous assessment and kept extremely detailed records. A key concern for her was breaking up the English curriculum in a way that fitted in with the pupils' developing understanding of issues while offering a clear progression in literacy with a scheme of work to follow. She was also very concerned that children should have both challenging literature and time to read old favourites. To this end, she was working with the LEA adviser to draw up lists of books suitable for each year group.

Subject knowledge for teaching literacy

In her questionnaire, Miss L differentiated clearly between the knowledge needed by beginning readers and writers and by those at Key Stage 2. At Key Stage 2, she specified that children should:

> read a range of challenging texts. Learn how to find information in books and make sure that they know how to evaluate books.

Writers needed to:

> use the right form for the purpose. Be clear about the content required for the audience and be able to manipulate the grammar and presentation conventions.

Miss L wrote on the questionnaire that she was much less confident about the knowledge needed by beginner readers and writers. In reading, she felt that they needed:

> to know how to handle books. That writing and pictures carry meaning and how, and that groups of letters make spoken words, and how they do it.

Writers needed:

> to know marks on paper communicate ideas, to link letters with sounds and to have something to say.

These views emphasise the importance of meaning and are consistent with Miss L's beliefs and practices. In the quiz, Miss L was able to identify nouns, verbs, adjectives, adverbs, pronouns, prepositions and articles, scoring 14, slightly higher than the median for effective teachers. She could identify some syllables and morphemes, but not phonemes, sounds or onset and rimes. She said that this concerned her, as she has been working with the school special educational needs co-ordinator to set up a phonics programme for some of her struggling readers and had felt quite confident in her understanding of phonics. Miss L was able to separate accent and dialect, and to discuss the differences between standard English and a dialect. She scored 22 on the Children's Author Recognition Test, rather better than the mean of 18 for the effective teachers. Miss L was very successful at identifying features and differences in the quiz samples of children's reading and writing. She identified content, detail and genre features first in the writing passage, then picked out the sentence structures, use of punctuation and spelling. In the reading, she identified all the errors and inferred cue use, drawing information from both the miscues and the retellings.

Common characteristics

Both of these teachers had characteristics in common – characteristics that we found to be widely shared by our sample of effective teachers of literacy. In summary, these were:

- Both valued their experiences in initial training and/or professional development, and particularly their roles as English co-ordinators, feeling that they had been given the opportunity and the motivation to reach a deeper understanding of good practice in teaching literacy.
- Both had made their classrooms highly literate environments, featuring attractive and stimulating displays of texts of various kinds. The features of these environments were heavily used by the children.
- Both used a shared text (read or written) as a vehicle for the teaching of specific aspects of reading and writing, e.g. phonics and spelling.
- Both deliberately brought out connections between the levels of language knowledge involved in reading or writing that text.
- Both were clear and focused about what they intended to teach.
- Both made clear to pupils the aims of the lesson and referred to these in the introductions and conclusions of lessons.

- Both emphasised the function of units of language in the context of an example of written language.
- Both used a mixture of whole class and group-based teaching in their lessons.
- Both taught lessons in which all children were engaged in literacy activities for the whole time.
- Both had planned literacy tasks that the whole class would eventually complete with appropriate support.
- Both had a strong belief in the priority of meaning making in teaching reading and writing.
- Both had a good knowledge of children's literature, but neither was able to segment sounds in the abstract context of a test.
- Both were very successful in identifying relevant features in samples of children's reading and writing.

Summary

In this chapter, we have exemplified some of the major findings emerging from the project by offering two detailed case studies of effective teachers of literacy. These teachers, like all our sample of effective teachers, were demonstrably effective in that they could demonstrate above-average literacy learning gains in the children they taught. We also observed them teach two literacy lessons, which were clearly very effective, the flavour of which we hope comes across in our descriptions.

7 Becoming an effective teacher of literacy

Introduction

We have described the ways in which the knowledge, beliefs and practices of the effective teachers of literacy in our study differed from those of a validation sample of teachers. One of the aims of the project was also to identify the origins of these underpinning factors. Consequently, we investigated the professional development experience of the effective teachers in our sample.

A number of types of data were collected to examine these issues. The questionnaires administered to the original 228 effective teachers of literacy and to the seventy-one members of the validation sample asked about qualifications and perceptions of professional development. In addition to this, those teachers we interviewed were asked about what had contributed to their development, both generally and with reference to particular teaching strategies and techniques. Both these sources of evidence indicated what the teachers themselves viewed as influential. Other factors, not perceived as important or given importance by the teachers, may also be significant. In addition to interviewing the teachers, we also interviewed the head-teachers of all the teachers in our sub-samples about their support for the development of these teachers' effectiveness in literacy teaching.

From this data, the following findings emerged as the most significant:

1 The effective teachers of literacy were more likely to have a subject background in English language and related subjects.
2 Experiences during initial teacher training had been largely forgotten by the effective experienced teachers, so little could be inferred about the quality of this training. The more recently qualified effective teachers, however, did value the training they had received in teaching literacy. This suggests that initial training had had an impact upon these teachers' approaches to and success in teaching literacy, but that this was inevitably short-term.
3 Experience of longer in-service courses and participation in long-term literacy projects had significantly affected teachers' views about literacy

teaching. The most significant feature of these longer-term experiences appeared to be that they had provided the opportunity and impetus for the teachers to develop and clarify their own personal philosophies about literacy teaching.

4 Shorter courses were also seen as useful in professional development, but largely in terms of meeting a personal need or keeping in touch with recent developments.

5 Effective teachers were more likely, and possibly more able, to discuss their views about literacy teaching as a philosophy and to make explicit links between their beliefs and their teaching practices.

6 The role of English co-ordinator was very significant to the effective teachers. It was a focus for in-service training provision of a certain type and had also generated substantial commitment to the area of teaching. Simply being the English co-ordinator meant that these teachers had experiences that involved them:

   • being perceived as experts by their colleagues;
   • being given the status of expert practitioner in teaching literacy in their schools;
   • being offered more extensive in-service course experiences in literacy;
   • having the chance to observe other teachers teach literacy, with a view to offering advice and support;
   • often being involved in delivering in-service training to their colleagues, with the consequent need to think actively through the material they were presenting.

7 Teachers not in the fortunate position of being the English co-ordinator in their school were more likely to be relatively deprived in terms of in-service training opportunities in literacy. Such deprivation seemed unlikely to enable these teachers to develop and increase their professional expertise in teaching literacy.

Teachers' subject backgrounds

There were some clear differences between the effective teachers and the validation teachers in terms of their subject backgrounds. A similar proportion of teachers in each group had qualifications at A level (71.1 per cent of effective teachers and 70.4 per cent of validation teachers), and the number of qualifications for each individual who had A levels was similar. However, 66.7 per cent of the effective teachers had A-level qualifications in subjects relevant to the content knowledge of literacy teaching (English, languages, linguistics and/or communication studies), while only 46.4 per cent of the validation teachers had such qualifications.

Of those teachers with degrees, 37.8 per cent of the effective teachers reported that the main subject of their degree was English, languages or linguistics, subjects likely to have relevance to the content knowledge of literacy teaching. Only 10.3 per cent of the validation sample listed these as their main degree subjects.

However, none of the teachers mentioned their A-level or degree studies as a source of professional development or preparation when interviewed. Whatever the longer-term effects of such subject backgrounds, the teachers themselves did not perceive them as very influential upon their subsequent teaching of literacy.

Initial teacher education

The general pattern of teaching qualifications of the teachers who filled in questionnaires reflected the age of the teachers in both samples, with the majority holding a Certificate of Education. Around a quarter of both samples had BEd or BA (QTS) degrees, with a smaller number having PGCE qualifications. There was little detectable difference between the two samples on this element.

Possibly because many of them had completed it so long ago, initial training was rarely reported by any of the teachers as an important feature in their development as teachers of literacy. The experienced teachers who mentioned their Initial Teacher Training (ITT) usually did so as a contrast to their later experience.

> When I first started teaching, because I didn't know how to teach reading it was a big worry for me. . . . The PLR [primary language record] was the thing, in about 1986. I was involved with the pilot and it made me think, really think, why am I doing all this? I don't think I am the sort of person that says there is only one way. I think I've always known there are lots of ways. I think what I'm convinced of now is that whatever way you use has got to be the one you believe in.

> I trained 20 years ago and at college they did not really teach us that you taught reading. You got this impression that the scheme did it – Ladybird. Then I was lucky enough to be involved in a conference. It was just like seeing the light. The fact you are making a role model . . . luckily I managed to get the other eight infant teachers interested and there was an excellent support network in Southampton then. We did not spend masses and masses of money on books, but we learned to use them differently. That conference and one on writing later were an inspiration. It was the professional assumption on somebody's part that we know what we are doing and why we are doing it.

In the sub-samples of teachers observed and interviewed, we deliberately included several with less than five years' experience. Some of the more recently qualified effective teachers of literacy did mention their initial teacher training courses, one to enthuse about the approach to teaching taken by a particular lecturer and another to praise the practical nature of the tasks she had undertaken during her PGCE English course. One of the validation sample also praised the practical nature of her initial training.

Professional development experience

A section of the questionnaire aimed to construct a picture of the sort of professional development the effective teachers of literacy had experienced and to compare this with that experienced by the validation teachers. We also invited teachers to offer views about the usefulness of the types of professional development in literacy that they had experienced and the literacy content included. Key features of what they said are reported in the following sections.

The duration of in-service experiences

Most of the teachers responding to the questionnaire had undertaken some in-service training focused on the teaching of literacy during the previous school year: 81 per cent of the effective teachers of literacy and 70.4 per cent of the validation teachers. The major difference between the two groups was in the number who had experienced substantial amounts of such in-service training: 16.8 per cent of the effective teachers of literacy had experienced more than five days, compared with only 2.8 per cent of the validation teachers.

At interview, all the effective teachers of literacy said that they undertook literacy-focused in-service training regularly and also participated in local support networks and literacy projects. They were also likely to belong to centres and support groups. Several mentioned long courses, such as 20-day Grant for Education Support and Training (GEST), diploma and masters' modules, as a significant influence on their practice, although these may have taken place some time ago. They suggested that such courses had given them opportunities to examine their assumptions about literacy carefully and relate them to their practice. Only one of the validation sample mentioned this type of professional development in literacy.

The effective teachers of literacy also said that they found regular attendance at shorter courses useful, but for different reasons. They suggested that these courses were likely to 'keep them up to date' and in contact with new requirements in literacy teaching, rather than offer a focus for examining their views and practices.

Source of in-service training experiences

Teachers were also asked in the questionnaire about the source of the literacy-related in-service training they had undertaken in the past year. Both groups had experienced in-service training organised by the school,

Table 7.1 The source of in-service training in literacy

Source of in-service training	Effective teachers who had experienced this (%)	Validation teachers who had experienced this (%)
School	72.2	81.7
LEA	74.9	66.2
Higher education	16.3	11.3
Distance learning	5.3	1.4

by the LEA, by a local university or college and through distance learning. The proportions of each group claiming to have experienced each of these types are shown in Table 7.1. These figures suggest that while many individuals in both samples had participated in a range of literacy-oriented in-service training opportunities, the effective teachers of literacy were more likely to have done in-service work organised from outside their schools. The validation teachers, on the other hand, tended to rely on school-based In-Serivce Education for Teachers provision.

The effective teachers generally talked positively about the LEA in-service training courses they had experienced.

> So I would say that the in-service courses [the LEA] run are excellent. They've got a good English team and I would say they have helped enormously. Some sessions are specifically for language co-ordinators, some for primary teachers in the borough. They come into school, the support team. They do really good practical sessions that we see the point of.

They also praised LEA-based support from advisers and advisory teachers within the school. The small number who had been involved with longer-term literacy courses at local universities also spoke enthusiastically about these.

Forms of professional development experience

The questionnaire also asked for teachers' views about a variety of types of provision for professional development in literacy. They were asked to say if they had experienced certain types of provision and to rate their usefulness. The forms of in-service training provision that they had experienced are shown in Table 7.2. The figures suggest that all the teachers had experienced a range of types of literacy in-service training provision but that the effective teachers were more likely to have taken part in literacy-related lectures, workshops and guided study. As these are often the features of out-of-school in-service training, this may relate to the finding in the previous

Table 7.2 The forms of in-service training experienced

Forms of in-service provision	Effective teachers who had experienced this (%)	Validation teachers who had experienced this (%)
Lectures	95.1	89.0
Practical workshops	92.3	86.2
Opportunities to try out new ideas in the classroom	98.7	98.5
Practical experience with feedback from an expert	75.8	67.2
Working alongside another teacher	77.2	73.0
In-service session led by colleagues	79.1	86.3
Observing other teachers in action	77.8	83.7
Guided research	63.3	43.9

section that the effective teachers were more likely to have experienced in-service training outside their schools. The validation teachers were more likely to have experienced in-service sessions led by colleagues and to have observed other teachers in action, both likely features of in-school provision.

The forms of professional development experience in literacy that teachers found very useful or useful are shown in Table 7.3. The figures indicate that the teachers who had experienced these forms of professional development had found most to be very useful or of some use. Trying out new ideas in the classroom was most likely to have been thought of use, with lectures least likely to be thought useful. The effective teachers who

Table 7.3 The forms of professional development experience found useful

Forms of professional development experience	Effective teachers rating this as very useful or useful (%)	Validation teachers rating this as very useful or useful (%)
Lectures	88.0	87.7
Practical workshops	95.0	94.6
Opportunities to try out new ideas in the classroom	99.1	100.0
Practical experience with feedback from an expert	98.8	93.4
Working alongside another teacher	95.2	93.6
In-service session led by colleagues	92.3	87.7
Observing other teachers in action	94.1	92.1
Guided research	90.4	72.0

had experienced in-service sessions led by colleagues were slightly less likely to find them useful. Given that these teachers are already effective, and that they experience proportionately less in-school literacy in-service training, this is perhaps not surprising. The validation teachers who had experienced guided research in literacy found it less useful than their effective colleagues, who were more likely to have engaged in it.

In addition to the types of in-service training listed in the questionnaire, we also asked teachers to list up to three other types of literacy professional development experience that had been useful to them. Comparatively few respondents named types of professional development: sixty-seven (29.4 per cent) of effective teachers and seven (9.9 per cent) validation teachers. However, the effective teachers named twenty-one types of literacy professional development that had been useful to them. The most mentioned of these were:

- personal reading about literacy (29.8 per cent of responses);
- discussion with colleagues (23.9 per cent);
- presenting in-service training sessions to colleagues (13.4 per cent);
- participation in national or local literacy projects (11.9 per cent of responses).

The validation teachers reported only three types of professional development:

- personal reading about literacy;
- participation in national/local literacy projects;
- visiting other schools.

This may suggest either that effective teachers of literacy participate in a wider range of types of professional development in literacy or that they are much more aware of their own professional development in literacy.

The content of professional development in literacy

In the questionnaire, we asked teachers to identify the areas of literacy teaching in which they felt their professional development had been particularly useful. In a list of nine content areas, teachers were asked to note those in which they had experienced professional development and to rate the usefulness of their experience of that content. Table 7.4 shows the percentage of both groups who had experienced professional development in each content area and the percentage who had found this useful. The figures indicate that, with the exception of the content areas 'assessment' and 'writing purposes and forms', the effective teachers were slightly more likely to have had professional development experience in these important aspects of literacy teaching and learning.

Table 7.4 The content of in-service training

Content area	Effective teachers who had experienced this (%)	Effective teachers rating this useful (%)	Validation teachers who had experienced this (%)	Validation teachers rating this useful (%)
Phonological awareness	86.3	87.4	77.1	91.4
Knowledge of grammar	84.4	66.5	72.2	65.9
Reading for information	94.4	90.9	85.7	83.3
Writing purposes and forms	96.9	98.6	97.1	93.7
Spelling development	92.1	90.0	80.0	86.5
Reading processes	96.2	95.8	91.0	91.7
Writing processes	97.8	97.2	92.3	96.7
Assessment	97.7	89.1	95.3	83.3
Children with literacy problems	90.6	85.3	82.8	88.6

The majority of teachers from both groups had found their professional development experience related to these topics useful, and there were no major differences between the two groups' ratings. The area that both groups seemed to have found less useful was *knowledge of grammar*.

To investigate these findings further, we probed teachers' responses to their in-service training during interview. The teachers did not find it easy to talk about the content of professional development in general questioning. Completion of the literacy quiz, however, did stimulate teachers to talk about their experience of work on grammar. Of the twenty-six effective teachers, twelve said that they felt they had learned the knowledge about language used for the quiz, in particular the word classes, but had been unable to retain this knowledge.

> I did know all this stuff. We did courses on it a few years back. You know, when it was, well, when the LEA were really keen on this sort of thing. Of course it was before I was into English so much. But I just don't use it, so of course it's gone. I don't know that I need it but I know that if I do need a particular word I can look it up. I've done that in the past, mostly when I taught juniors. I make really sure I know what I'm talking about before I do it with the kids. It's like the science now, isn't it?

> I was OK on it straight after the course, but it is impossible to remember for some reason. I really believe it's because it simply isn't how we do it in class. I mean, if I get ideas from a course. Or if the content of

a course is really relevant to school I do use it. I was very interested when I did that KAL (knowledge about language) course because I felt I improved my own knowledge. But this detail is not the sort of thing I would use in class or the others [other teachers] are going to benefit from me bringing back.

I remember doing all this at secondary school. It was so boring then and I haven't used it since, so of course I am a bit out of practice. I do know what I need for the classroom but I wouldn't feel this is relevant to me at KS1 now so that's probably why.

Most of the validation teachers gave very similar explanations for their feelings about what they recognised as their difficulties with the content of the quiz. Two of these teachers said that they had had a good grounding in this sort of thing at school and they felt that it had been useful to them in their teaching, although they did not do noticeably better on the quiz than the others. Two others of the validation sample said they felt that they needed help in this area and that it would improve their teaching if they knew more about grammar.

The results of the questionnaire and the comments made by teachers suggest two main problems with training courses about knowledge about language or about grammar. First, teachers may fail to perceive the relationship between explicit content at their own level, in areas such as grammar, and the material they see as important for them to teach. Second, if, as our data indicates, effective teachers tend to teach areas such as sentence-level work within the context of work on whole texts, they may not make the connection between the grammatical knowledge they are taught on courses and the classroom activities they are accustomed to employ. In-service courses on grammar would seem more likely to have a longer-term impact if they were planned with these connections deliberately in mind.

When the teachers were asked during the interviews what experiences had helped them to develop their literacy teaching, the results were very different for the effective and validation teachers. In some ways this is to be expected, since the validation teachers were all mathematics co-ordinators and a high proportion of the effective teachers were English co-ordinators. However, some broad differences are striking.

Two of the validation teachers said that they did not see themselves as teachers of literacy, and others suggested that they did not feel they could be effective in the literacy field as they were mathematics co-ordinators. Given the responsibilities of a primary teacher for the whole curriculum, such a view is, of course, untenable.

Although all the effective teachers were able to talk about their development, they all found it difficult to relate particular factors in this to their current teaching practice. They named many more factors in their development and were much more likely, for example, to talk about their personal philosophies of literacy teaching. A number could name turning points in their development as literacy teachers that related to this personal philosophy. These fell into a number of categories:

- particular courses they had attended;
- particular course techniques (particularly a practical approach);
- particular materials or the need for new materials forcing them to review their approach.

It was notable that many of the Key Stage 1 effective teachers made long comments about particular reading materials and phonic programmes to explain why they did or did not fit into the way they taught. This often seemed to be a real focus for strong feeling about theoretical issues. In particular, they questioned the extent to which children learned to apply the phonic rules they were working with in published phonic programmes. This criticism links to the finding described earlier that these teachers tended to teach phonics in relation to larger units of text.

Becoming the school English co-ordinator

One of the most important factors in the development of the effective teachers of literacy was undoubtedly becoming the school English co-ordinator.

> Taking on the role of co-ordinator. I've tended to. I've thought to myself, 'well, I'm going to find out more' so I've read more, I've looked into things more and, I can't say when it happened, I've started to look more at what the child can do. I think I take into account more what the child has to do, the skills they need. In my first few years I probably would have introduced things but not been aware of the skills the child would need.

They gave a number of possible reasons why this was significant:

- Support from school colleagues.

> Being part of staff teams who are open to new ideas but analysed them for me before we actually got on any bandwagon. We had people who were deliberately devil's advocate. I remember when we were going for a new approach at my previous school. We talked about it at length, got in advisers who helped us and sorted it out amongst ourselves, but there was not one person who just said 'Oh the old fashioned ways are the best'. Luckily, I've always worked with people who want to know what's best and form their own opinions.

- Being able to see what colleagues in and out of school did in class – something they felt would only be possible for the co-ordinator.

> I think it's the opportunity to go and see other people doing it. From being English co-ordinator and having responsibility for something. Once a term we have a day for us. I mean it might be doing files and paperwork. But on the other hand I do like to try and go and see other people. You do pick up ideas of how to do things. I've learned a lot more about Y3 and their abilities from going over to the infant school and seeing Y2. I'm Key Stage 2 trained but seeing the ways they read and their sessions and the stimulus in the classroom. I try to recreate that in my teaching.

- Becoming part of a network of co-ordinators who kept in touch with each other.
- Receiving regular bulletins and support from county advisory staff and services.
- Personal interest.
- Becoming involved with initiatives such as the Primary Language Record or literacy projects.

There did seem to be a great difference in the type, duration, content and forms of continuing professional development offered to English co-ordinators and to other teachers in the schools we visited. One teacher expressed her concern about this issue.

> But I'm afraid it's all gone wrong, because the only courses you get to go on are consultant courses. I'm finding that as the language consultant I'm expected to go on courses concerned with language but the other members of staff don't get those opportunities, whereas I feel when I was younger I could go on any courses I wanted. So I'm concerned that they're not doing enough basic in-service about language.

Such a concern, if accurate (and the evidence of our research is that is does represent a common pattern), suggests a worrying 'vicious circle' in the professional development experience of teachers who are not English co-ordinators for their schools (with, naturally, a parallel 'virtuous circle' for those who *are*). Teachers who do not exhibit particular strengths in the teaching of literacy, and who are therefore unlikely to be selected as English co-ordinators, are less likely to be given access to the in-service training experiences that can help them to strengthen their teaching of literacy. If an aim of continuing professional development is to try to make *all* primary teachers effective teachers of literacy, then this feature of course provision seems to need some attention.

Other factors

At interview, many of the teachers offered very general explanations of their development as effective teachers of literacy and were unable to select the significant factors.

> Well, mainly by watching other teachers I suppose. Certainly, since I've been here I've had the opportunity to watch other teachers working and have picked up things from them otherwise – experience. Trying things out as you go along and finding certain things work and developing them really.

> I do read a lot of things. I read a lot of research and the *Times Ed.* and I see what everyone else is doing and I like trying out different things to see what works for me.

> A combination of seeing other teachers teach, reading books and experimenting in my class to see what works best. So there's no one single factor, it's what works best. It's mostly articles and stuff I read these days, although I do look at the books I had when I trained six years ago. I had a Margaret Meek one that really influenced me.

When probed about the important aspects of their professional development in the last academic year, the effective teachers of literacy were more likely to identify a particular course, school-based session or the opportunity to discuss school-based matters with colleagues. The validation teachers were more likely to identify the support of another member of staff and the opportunity to talk to other members of staff.

Headteachers' support for teachers of literacy

The eighteen headteachers of the twenty-six effective teachers and ten validation teachers were interviewed about these teachers. They cited a number of experiences that had contributed to the effectiveness of their colleagues, the most frequently mentioned in the case of the effective teachers of literacy being INSET outside school or participation in projects about literacy. For the validation teachers, the most frequently mentioned factor was advice from colleagues in various forms. This difference fits with the evidence from the teachers themselves that they had been most affected by external INSET or involvement in projects (effective teachers) or school-based INSET (validation teachers).

The headteachers also identified measures they had taken to support their colleagues' professional development as teachers of literacy. These were all factors identified by the teachers as important to their professional development, although individual headteachers did not necessarily choose the same factors as the teachers. In the case of the effective teachers, the most frequently mentioned measures were in-school structures such as staff meetings and working parties (mentioned by 30.7 per cent of the heads of the effective teachers) and arrangements for teachers to undertake out-of-school meetings such as co-ordinators' meetings and in-service training courses (26.9 per cent). The heads of validation teachers were generally more vague about supporting their staff member in literacy, with 54.5 per cent mentioning school events such as whole school planning and policy making.

Summary

From our study of these teachers, a clear distinction emerged between the effective teachers of literacy and the validation teachers in terms of the professional development experiences they had had. In general, the effective teachers had been offered opportunities, beyond those provided in school, to extend and develop their knowledge and expertise in the teaching of literacy. For the validation teachers, these opportunities tended to have been limited to those provided in school. Much of this difference can be accounted for by the fact that most of the effective teachers of literacy we studied were, or had been, English co-ordinators in their schools, a position of relative privilege in terms of access to literacy-focused professional development. The clear implication of this finding is that, to raise expertise levels in all teachers of literacy, some professional development opportunities at least need to be channelled to those teachers not already identified as expert.

8 Conclusions and implications

Introduction

In this chapter, we shall present the conclusions arising from this research project and then outline what we perceive to be the major implications for future policy and practice. Our findings are based on close examination of the work of a sample of teachers whose pupils make effective learning gains in literacy and of a more random sample of teachers whose pupils make less progress in literacy.

We will begin by outlining the conclusions of the research in the order in which they were presented in previous chapters. We will then try to synthesise these conclusions into an overall interpretation of our main findings about the characteristics of effective teachers of literacy before going on to discuss the implications of our work for continuing professional development and future research.

Conclusions: a restatement

The teaching practices of effective teachers of literacy

- There were some differences between the reading activities likely to be employed by the effective teachers and the teachers in the validation group. The effective teachers made more use of big books in their teaching; they were also more likely to use other adults to assist their classroom work. The validation teachers made more use of phonic exercises and flashcards, although both groups were similar in the extent to which they reported and were observed to teach letter sounds. The difference was in the ways they went about this. The effective teachers tended to teach letter sounds within the context of using a text (often a big book) and to use short, regular teaching sessions, often involving them modelling to the children how sounds worked (by, for example, writing examples of letter groups on a flipchart). The validation teachers were much more likely to approach letter-sound teaching through the use of paper exercises.

- The effective teachers were generally much more likely to embed their teaching of reading into a wider context and to show how specific aspects of reading and writing contribute to communication. They tended to use whole texts as the basis from which to teach skills such as vocabulary, word attack and recognition, and use of text features. They were also very clear about their purposes in using such texts.

- In lessons involving writing, the differences between the two groups of teachers were less clear, although it did seem that the effective teachers were more likely to use published teaching materials as a way of consolidating the language points they had already taught their children, whereas for the validation teachers, these materials were often used to introduce a teaching session. This suggests that a similar point to that made about reading work also applies in the case of writing work. The effective teachers generally tried to ensure that their teaching of language features was contextualised for their children and that the children understood the purpose of this teaching. Their chief means of achieving such contextualisation was to focus teaching on a shared text. Language features were taught, and explained to the children, as a means of managing this shared text rather than as a set of rules or definitions to be learned for their own sakes.

- The effective teachers of literacy, because of their concern to contextualise their teaching of language features within shared text experiences, made explicit connections for their pupils between the text, sentence and word levels of language study.

- The lessons of the effective teachers were all conducted at a brisk pace. They regularly refocused children's attention on the task at hand and used clear time frames to keep children on task. They also tended to conclude their lessons by reviewing, with the whole class, what the children had done during the lesson. Lessons that ended with the teacher simply saying 'We'll finish this tomorrow' were much more common among the validation teachers.

- The effective teachers used modelling extensively. They regularly demonstrated reading and writing to their classes in a variety of ways, often accompanying these demonstrations by verbal explanations of what they were doing. In this way, they were able to make available to the children their thinking as they engaged in literacy.

- Some effective teachers differentiated the work they asked pupils to do by allotting different tasks on the basis of ability. These teachers also used another approach by varying the support given to particular groups of children when they were engaged on tasks that the whole class would do at some point. By this means, they were able to keep their classes working more closely together through a programme of work.

- The classrooms of the effective teachers were distinguished by the heavy emphasis on literacy in the environments that had been created. There were many examples of literacy displayed in these classrooms, these examples were regularly brought to the children's attentions, and the children were encouraged to use them to support their own literacy.

- The effective teachers had very clear assessment procedures, usually involving a great deal of focused observation and systematic record keeping. This contributed markedly to their abilities to select appropriate literacy content for their children's needs.

Teachers' subject knowledge in literacy

- All the teachers we worked with knew the requirements of the National Curriculum well and recognised the different literacy teaching needs of Key Stage 1 and Key Stage 2 children.
- There were differences between the validation sample and the effective teachers in their specifications of what children needed to know about reading and writing. The effective teachers in general placed a greater emphasis on children's recognition of the purposes and functions of reading and writing and of the structures used to enable these processes. The validation teachers, on the other hand, were more likely to emphasise technical knowledge about these structures. This should not be taken to imply that the effective teachers gave less attention to language structures in their teaching but rather that they were more concerned to contextualise their teaching of these and to present them functionally and meaningfully to children.
- All the teachers had limited success in recognising some types of word in a sentence and some sub-word units out of context. The effective teachers were more likely to be able to pick out word types such as adjectives, adverbs, etc. but less able to identify such units as phonemes, onsets and rimes, and morphemes. Using more everyday terminology for these units still did not ensure total success for the teachers in recognising them. This casts doubt on the effective teachers' abstract knowledge of linguistic concepts such as 'phoneme' and raises the question of whether they would be even more effective if they had such knowledge.
- Despite this apparent lack of explicit, abstract knowledge of linguistic concepts, these teachers were observed to use such knowledge implicitly in their teaching, particularly that connected with phonics. Our interpretation of this contradiction is that the effective teachers knew the material they were teaching in a particular way. It did not seem to be the case that the teachers selected appropriate ways to represent (pedagogy) pre-existing knowledge (content) to children. Rather, they appeared to know and understand the material in the form in which they taught it to the children, which was usually as material that helped these children to read and write. The effective teachers' knowledge about content and their knowledge about teaching and learning strategies

were integrated. The knowledge base of these teachers was thus their pedagogical content knowledge.

- When examining and judging samples of children's reading and writing, all the teachers were able to analyse mistakes, but the way in which the two groups approached the task was different:
  - The effective teachers were more diagnostic in the ways they approached the task and were more able to generate explanations as to why children read or wrote as they did.
  - In examining the pieces of writing, the two groups eventually mentioned similar features, but the effective teachers were quicker to focus on possible underlying causes of a child's writing behaviour.
  - The validation sample required lots of prompting and time to reach an equivalent point. It is likely that, in a busy classroom context, they would not routinely make the same level of judgements made by the effective teachers.
- We also found that the teachers used a limited range of linguistic terminology, and the way the two groups of teachers used this terminology was different. The validation teachers tended to rely on definitions of the terms they used, whereas the effective teachers tended to begin by demonstrating particular language features in use within a clear context before deriving a definition, which might well be arrived at in discussion with the children. Children in the classes of these teachers were thus much more heavily involved in problem solving and theorising about language for themselves rather than simply being given 'facts' to learn.

The belief systems of effective teachers of literacy

- The effective teachers of literacy tended to place a high value upon communication and composition in their views about the teaching of reading and writing; that is, they believed that the creation of meaning in literacy was fundamental. They were more coherent in their belief systems about the teaching of literacy and tended to favour teaching activities that explicitly emphasised the deriving and creating of meaning. In much of their teaching, they were at pains to stress to pupils the purposes and functions of reading and writing tasks.
- Although they emphasised purpose and meaning in their belief statements, this did not mean that the more technical aspects of reading and writing processes were neglected. There was plenty of evidence that such aspects as phonic knowledge, spelling, grammatical knowledge and punctuation were prominent in the teaching of effective teachers of literacy. Technical aspects of literacy, however, tended to be approached in quite different ways by the effective teachers than by most of the teachers in the validation sample.
- The key difference in approach was in the effective teachers' emphasis on embedding attention to word- and sentence-level aspects of reading

and writing within whole text activities that were both meaningful and explained clearly to pupils. Teachers in the validation sample were more likely to teach technical features as discrete skills for their own sakes and did not necessarily ensure that pupils understood the wider purpose of such skills in reading and writing.

- Our finding concerning the beliefs of this group of effective teachers of literacy, that they prioritised the creation of meaning in their literacy teaching, thus reflects not that they failed to emphasise such skills as phonics, spelling, grammar, etc. but rather that they were trying very hard to ensure that such skills were developed in children with a clear eye to the children's awareness of their importance and function.

Professional development issues

- The effective teachers of literacy were more likely to have a subject background in English language or related subjects.
- Experiences during initial teacher training had now been largely forgotten by the effective experienced teachers, so little could be inferred about the quality of this training. The more recently qualified effective teachers, however, did value the training they had received in teaching literacy. This suggests that initial training does have an important impact upon teachers' approaches to and success at teaching literacy, but that this is inevitably short-term.
- Experience of longer in-service courses and participation in long-term literacy projects had significantly affected teachers' views about literacy teaching. The most significant feature of these longer-term experiences appeared to be that they had provided the opportunity and impetus for the teachers to develop and clarify their own personal philosophies about literacy teaching.
- Shorter courses were also seen as useful in professional development, but largely in terms of meeting a personal need or keeping in touch with recent developments.
- Effective teachers were more likely, and possibly more able, to discuss their views about literacy teaching as a philosophy and to make explicit links between their beliefs and their teaching practices.
- The role of English co-ordinator was very significant to the effective teachers. It was a focus for in-service training provision of a certain type and had also generated substantial commitment to the area of teaching. Simply being the English co-ordinator meant that these teachers had experiences that involved them:
  - being perceived as experts by their colleagues;
  - being given the status of expert practitioner in teaching literacy in their schools;
  - being offered more extensive in-service training course experiences in literacy;

- having the chance to observe other teachers teach literacy, with a view to offering advice and support;
- often being involved in delivering in-service training to their colleagues, with the consequent need to think through actively the material they were presenting.
- Teachers not in the fortunate position of being the English co-ordinator in their school were more likely to be relatively deprived in terms of in-service training opportunities in literacy. Such deprivation is unlikely to enable these teachers to develop and increase their professional expertise in teaching literacy.

An interpretation of these conclusions

Our analysis of a wide range of data concerning the teachers we identified as effective teachers of literacy produced a relatively consistent picture of the characteristics of these teachers and the factors underpinning these characteristics.

Broadly speaking, it seemed that the effective teachers of literacy placed a great deal of emphasis on presenting literacy to their children in ways that foregrounded the creation and recreation of meaning. Because meaning was such a high priority, they tried wherever possible to embed their teaching of the crucial technical features of literacy (how to do it) in a context where the children could see why they were learning about such features. This context very often involved the use of a shared text, which was being either read or written together. As this text was being either read or written, the fundamental skills and features involved were being taught systematically by the teachers: for example, phonics, spelling, grammar, punctuation, textual structures and conventions. The teachers were thus continually making connections explicit for their pupils between text-, sentence- and word-level language features. These features were thus taught in a way that emphasised their functions in language rather than their focus being simply a set of rules and definitions to learn.

This functional approach also reflects the form that these teachers' knowledge about written language features took and it seemed that, rather than having learned about these features *then* tried to find ways of presenting them to their children, they knew them in the ways they taught them – as features that enable written language to be produced and interpreted.

Another characteristic of these teachers' approach to literacy teaching was the explicitness with which they set about it. They demonstrated a great deal of literacy to children, modelling the processes of reading and writing but also at the same time explaining the thinking underlying these activities. In this way, the children were being helped to become more explicitly aware of why and how they could read and write successfully.

The teachers themselves were very aware of how they were teaching literacy and had generally made very reasoned decisions about this. Many of them had developed strong personal philosophies about literacy teaching, and these had come about through a willingness, and the opportunity, to reflect on their practice and the nature of what they were teaching. These opportunities resulted from prolonged study, involvement in literacy projects and/or curriculum responsibility for English in their schools.

Finally, the effective teachers were thoroughly systematic in the ways they went about their teaching of literacy. They were very familiar with the requirements of the National Curriculum for English and had worked out, with their schools, systems of teaching that enabled them to guarantee appropriate coverage of these requirements. Although a feature of effective teachers' practice, such systems were also used by other teachers, although as a determinant of school planning. The effective teachers were also likely to use diagnostic information about children, their development and literacy progression as a planning tool. They had well-developed systems for gathering evidence concerning children's progress and needs in literacy and using this to inform detailed planning for future teaching. Such a diagnostic approach often led them to tailor the support they offered to particular children, or groups of children, to ensure that, as far as possible, the whole class covered similar ground in literacy.

In the context of recent developments in the teaching of literacy, in particular, the experience of the National Literacy Project (and its broadening into the National Literacy Strategy) and the National Curriculum for Initial Teacher Training, it is important to point out how close most of our effective teachers of literacy were to the model of literacy teaching implied in these developments. The following points are central to this:

- The effective teachers of literacy had an extensive knowledge of the content of literacy, even though this was not generally a knowledge that could be abstracted from the context of their teaching action.
- Because of this knowledge they were able to see, and help their pupils to see, connections between the text, sentence and word levels of language.
- The effective teachers had coherent belief systems about literacy and its teaching, and these were generally consistent with the ways they chose to teach.
- These belief systems, and hence their teaching practices, tended to emphasise the importance of children being clear about the purposes of reading and writing and of using this clarity of purpose as a means of embedding the teaching of grammar, phonics, etc. into contexts that made sense to the children.
- These teachers were teaching literacy in lessons that were clearly focused on this 'subject' and that bore remarkable resemblance to the literacy hours now commonplace in primary schools. In these lessons, they used a mixture of whole class interactive teaching and small group guided work, with occasional individual teaching usually undertaken by a classroom assistant or volunteer helper.

- A good deal of their teaching involved the use of shared texts such as big books, duplicated passages and multiple copies of books, through which the attention of a whole class or group was drawn to text-, sentence- and word-level features. The ways in which they were making connections between different levels of language knowledge accorded generally with the framework developed in the National Literacy Project (National Literacy Project, 1997), in which it is suggested that 'text level work provides the essential context for much of the work at the sentence and word levels'.

Implications for further development

Several implications emerge from this research in terms of future policy and practice in continuing professional development. These concern the following:

- access to in-service training courses;
- the nature of professional development experience;
- the content of in-service training courses;
- the nature and content of initial training;
- the role of the subject co-ordinator in the school.

Access to in-service training courses

Over a number of years now there has been a tendency for literacy curriculum specialists (school English co-ordinators) to be targeted for in-service training opportunities in literacy. The priorities identified in the annual GEST funding, for example, have been echoed by LEA provision. This targeting has been implemented for very good reasons. There were clear needs, following the introduction of the National Curriculum, for a heightening of subject expertise and for ensuring that at least one member of staff in a school was sufficiently expert and knowledgeable about the teaching of a subject to be able to offer support and advice to colleagues in this teaching.

There is some evidence from our findings that this policy of targeting in-service training opportunities has had a positive effect. The effective teachers of literacy in our sample, over 70 per cent of whom were English co-ordinators for their schools, consistently reported having benefited from the in-service training opportunities available to them. They claimed to have been able to pass on some of their expertise through running or organising in-school training sessions for their colleagues and through offering general support to these colleagues in such areas as selecting resources for literacy and implementing school policies.

Our evidence does suggest, however, that a rather worrying corollary of this policy has been that teachers who had not been designated as school

English co-ordinators were somewhat restricted in the in-service training opportunities available to them. For many, these were limited to those arranged within the school, during after-school sessions or on occasional school training days. Given the high value that the effective teachers placed upon their experiences of in-service training courses, it seems that non-specialists were missing out on opportunities for their expertise in teaching literacy to be improved. There is a 'Matthew effect' in operation here: the rich (in literacy expertise) tend to get richer, while the poor (perhaps a majority of primary teachers) fall further and further behind the most up-to-date thinking and practice. This does not seem a satisfactory state of affairs. It is true, after all, that *all* primary teachers are teachers of literacy and, especially in the case of younger children, have an enormous responsibility for ensuring appropriate literacy development in children. Thus it seems to follow that *all* teachers need professional development in this crucial area.

The nature of professional development experience

Two points stand out in this area. First, we have some evidence of the benefits in developing and strengthening teaching expertise in literacy of teachers being brought together in structured discussion groups. These often took the form of regular meetings between teachers from a range of professional situations to discuss particular issues in literacy teaching, and a prime example of such meetings was the English co-ordinators' groups that several of our effective teachers belonged to. Working in such groups also sometimes involved watching other teachers teach, and being watched teaching in turn. There is evidence from other sources of the positive benefits of such support groups. For example, they were at the heart of the success of the Extending Literacy (EXEL) project (Wray and Lewis, 1994) in developing and spreading expertise in extending children's work with non-fiction texts. They were also vital to the success of national projects such as the National Writing Project and, later, the National Oracy Project. This approach to professional development might be more widely adopted if part of the funds dedicated to continuing professional development were earmarked to support such structured groups, perhaps by allowing teachers to be released occasionally from their class responsibilities to take part in meetings with other teachers for specific purposes.

Second, a number of the effective teachers of literacy had experienced involvement either in long courses about the teaching of literacy, such as CAPS or MEd courses, or in literacy projects, such as the development and trialling of the Primary Language Record. These experiences, as well as having given these teachers access to sources of extensive expertise, both personal and resource-based, had also given them the time and space to reflect in a structured way upon their own approaches to literacy teaching and to develop their personal philosophies. Where teachers had worked out philosophies regarding literacy and its teaching, these did seem to act positively as a co-ordinating force in their day-to-day practices, and this co-ordination in turn led to increased focus in the literacy teaching adopted. Clearly, involving more teachers in longer courses and study programmes in literacy has very significant resource implications and may not be possible to the degree to which might be thought ideal. In fact, there has been a marked decrease over a twenty-year period in the number of teachers released from their schools for longer periods of study. What is more feasible, and has emerged as a professional development policy quite recently, is the deliberate facilitation and encouragement of teachers who want to involve themselves more fully in educational research. Such a move towards teaching as an enquiry-based profession is plainly justified by the findings of our research.

The content of in-service training courses

The effective teachers in this study reported that they found in-service courses on such topics as grammar less useful than courses on other topics. This is indicative of a more general implication of the research that the most effective in-service training content is not that which focuses on knowledge at the teachers' own level but rather that which deals with subject knowledge in terms of how this is taught to children. Our suggestion earlier was that subject knowledge in literacy should not be conceived as knowledge of content, which the teacher then had to decide how to represent to children. Instead, it seems from our research that effective teachers of literacy know the content of literacy as pedagogy; that is, they represent the knowledge to themselves through the ways they teach it.

If this is correct, then it suggests that the most effective in-service training courses in literacy will be those that focus on the teaching of literacy content and aim to extend the range of pedagogic strategies at a teacher's disposal. This implies a more practical approach, and the teachers in this study confirmed that one of the most successful forms of in-service training was that which gave them opportunities to try out new ideas in the classroom. However, this does not mean that in-service training courses should be *only* practical – that is, entirely classroom-based. In aiming to develop teachers' ability to teach literacy more effectively, they should be mindful of the importance, discussed earlier, of the teacher as a reflective professional. The more teachers are themselves aware of the underpinnings, theoretical and philosophical, of how they act in classrooms, the more likely they are to take a coherent approach to their literacy teaching that seems to pay most dividends. Thus there has to be a place in an in-service training course, however practical its focus, for teachers to debate and work out the place of practical ideas in their personal, reasoned armoury of teaching strategies.

Another issue arising from our finding about the relatively low effectiveness of in-service training courses on grammar concerns the role of linguistic terminology for teachers. While we found little evidence that the effective teachers of literacy had an extensive command of a range of linguistic terminology, it does seem at least possible that having a greater command might help them to improve their teaching of literacy further. Having the linguistic terms available might enable then to be more precise in their explanations to children. Certainly, without knowing appropriate terminology, teachers often have to invent ways of describing linguistic phenomena to their children. To quote the Kingman Report (DES, 1988): 'there is no positive advantage in such ignorance' (p. 4), and it might be useful to find ways of increasing teacher knowledge in this area. However, in view of the findings of the project, we would strongly recommend that such terminology be introduced (or reintroduced) to teachers not as a set of definitions for them to learn but as the embodiments of linguistic functions with a strong emphasis upon the ways these functions might be taught.

Our suggestion as a first step towards increasing knowledge of linguistic terms and associated functions is to take a route that does seem to have had some demonstrable success already. In talking to the teachers in our samples, both the effective and the validation teachers, it quickly became quite plain that they were almost all very comfortable with the language used in the current requirements for the English National Curriculum. Familiarity with the terms of these requirements has clearly been a necessity for primary teachers as they have legally had to fulfil them. This suggests that embedding a more extensive range of linguistic terminology in other equivalent official documents may well have the effect of ensuring a greater awareness of this terminology, as long as this terminology is described in functional terms.

The nature and content of initial training

The above comments regarding in-service training courses in literacy generally also apply to initial training in literacy. A priority here must be equipping novice teachers with a range of pedagogic strategies to enable them to operate successfully in developing children's literacy. But, as with experienced teachers, developing such strategies involves more than simple practical experience. Novice teachers also need to develop an awareness of why and in what circumstances they might employ particular teaching approaches. They need not only procedural knowledge about literacy teaching (knowing how) but also conditional knowledge (knowing when and in what way). The development of this knowledge seems to demand experience in a range of contrasting contexts, together with the opportunity to compare and contrast their experiences with those of others. It would also be useful for them to be taught specific strategies and then be given the opportunity to try these out under guidance in classrooms.

Beginning teachers, if they are to move quickly towards becoming effective teachers of literacy, also need to be given the opportunity and the space to develop their own philosophies of literacy teaching. There is evidence that initial training courses do allow student teachers to 'make their own minds up' about approaches to the teaching of reading (Wray and Medwell, 1994).

As discussed above, the effective teachers in our sample were very likely to have experienced some form of involvement with a project on an aspect of literacy teaching. The opportunity to think through issues while working towards a practical outcome appeared to have enabled them to develop more coherent personal philosophies about literacy teaching. It would therefore seem likely to be beneficial if initial training courses could engage students at some point in such project-based learning, perhaps a small-scale research study, in an aspect of literacy teaching. Many courses already make provision for this on a limited scale, but there is evidence (Wray, 1993) that student teachers respond very well to involvement in more elaborate research projects.

The role of the subject co-ordinator in the school

The evidence from this project suggests that, in order to become an effective teacher of literacy, one of the most beneficial steps that a teacher could take is to become the English co-ordinator in his/her school. This puts the teacher into the position of:

- receiving more extensive opportunities for professional development;
- having the opportunity to learn from explaining ideas to other teachers and from watching other teachers teach;
- being vested with an expertise that they then have to live up to;
- being the gate-keeper in the school for new ideas and resources.

Such a position strongly encourages the development of specialist expertise, and one suggestion for a way of broadening the possession of this expertise would be for schools to rotate the role of English co-ordinator every few years. In several of the schools we visited as part of the project, such rotation of responsibilities was already practised, and the teachers involved were certainly building up their range of curriculum expertise. In one school, for example, four teachers were identified as effective teachers of literacy. Of these, one was the current English co-ordinator, two had held this post in the past (they were now responsible for other curriculum areas), and one was in her second year of teaching. Rotation of responsibilities (and of year groups taught) was a deliberate school policy and seemed to be having the desired effect of spreading expertise.

Conclusion

In this research, a fairly coherent picture has emerged of the characteristics of effective teachers. We feel that there are also some clear implications for policy and practice and have tried to outline these in this chapter. Many of these centre on what might be referred to as a functionalist approach to the teaching of literacy, and we see this as our most significant finding. If adopted more widely, we feel that this approach has the potential to enhance significantly teachers' expertise and hence children's learning in literacy.

Appendix A: Background details of teachers involved in the project

- Of the 228 effective teachers, 213 (95.5 per cent) were female and ten male (4.5 per cent). In the validation sample, 54 (77.1 per cent) were female and sixteen (22.9 per cent) were male.
- The age profile for both samples was very similar, with most of the teachers aged 40–49. There were 122 (54 per cent) effective teachers in this age group and 38 (53.5 per cent) validation teachers. In both samples, there were similar numbers of teachers above and below this age range and very few teachers under 25.
- The groups also had a similar experience profile, with most of the teachers (71.7 per cent of effective teachers and 67.6 per cent of the validation teachers) having had more than ten years teaching experience.
- 55.3 per cent of the effective teachers of literacy taught in infant classes, and 44.3 per cent taught junior or Y7 classes. 29.8 per cent of them taught classes of more than one year group and 4.4 per cent the Y2/Y3 transitional age group. Of the validation teachers, 43.6 per cent taught in infant classes and 66.2 per cent in junior or Y7 classes. 43.7 per cent of these teachers taught mixed-age classes and 9.9 per cent across the key stages.
- The teachers in both samples were likely to have taught a range of year groups in the last five years. 33.3 per cent of the effective teachers of literacy had changed key stage from infants to juniors/Y7 or *vice versa*. 42 per cent of the validation teachers had changed.
- Only 5.7 per cent of the effective teachers of literacy were headteachers, whereas 18.3 per cent of the validation teachers were headteachers. All of these were teaching heads. 24.6 per cent of the effective teachers of literacy were teaching deputy heads, compared with 15.5 per cent of the validation teachers.
- Of the effective teachers of literacy, 70.1 per cent held or had held curriculum co-ordination responsibility for English, with 50.4 per cent continuing to do so. 12.7 per cent of the validation teachers also co-ordinated or had co-ordinated English in their schools, with 4.2 per cent continuing to do so, presumably in conjunction with their mathematics co-ordination role.

Appendix B: Questionnaire administered to all teachers in the project

Section 1: Background information

Q1   Are you Male ☐
Female ☐

Q2   Are you Under 25 ☐
25–29 ☐
30–39 ☐
40–49 ☐
50–59 ☐
Over 60 ☐

Q3   How many years teaching experience had you had at the start of this school year?

None ☐
1 year ☐
2–5 years ☐
6–10 years ☐
More than 10 years ☐

Q4   If you studied A levels before your teacher training course, please write in the subjects you passed.

Q5   What type of teacher training course did you take?

BEd ☐
PGCE ☐
Cert. Ed. ☐
Articled teacher ☐
Licensed teacher ☐
Other (please specify)

Q6   How many years of study did this involve?

Q7   When did you qualify as a teacher?

Which of the following qualifications do you hold? For each, write in the main subject(s).

Q8   BA ☐
Q9   BSc ☐
Q10   BEd ☐

Q11   MA   ☐
Q12   MEd   ☐
Q13   MPhil   ☐
Q14   MSc   ☐
Q15   PhD   ☐
Q16   Other (please specify)
Q17   Which year group(s) are you teaching this year?
Q18   Which year group(s) have you taught during the past five years?
       Tick any positions of responsibility you currently hold or have held
       in the past.
Q19   Headteacher   ☐
Q20   Deputy head   ☐
Q21   English/Language co-ordinator   ☐
Q22   Other co-ordinator (please specify)

Section 2: Professional development experience

Q23   How many days in-service training focused upon the teaching of
       reading/writing have you undertaken during the last school year?
       Which of the following have you experienced during this year?
Q24   In-service training in your school   ☐
Q25   In-service training organised by the LEA   ☐
Q26   In-service training by distance learning   ☐
Q27   In-service training at a university or college   ☐

       Which forms of professional development do you feel have been
       particularly useful in developing your teaching of literacy? Tick
       according to the following: Very useful = 1; Of some use = 2; Not
       very useful = 3; I have not experienced this = 4.
Q28   Lectures   1 ☐ 2 ☐ 3 ☐ 4 ☐
Q29   Practical workshops   1 ☐ 2 ☐ 3 ☐ 4 ☐
Q30   Opportunities to try out new ideas in
       the classroom   1 ☐ 2 ☐ 3 ☐ 4 ☐
Q31   Practical experience with feedback from
       an expert   1 ☐ 2 ☐ 3 ☐ 4 ☐
Q32   Working alongside another teacher   1 ☐ 2 ☐ 3 ☐ 4 ☐
Q33   In-service sessions led by colleagues   1 ☐ 2 ☐ 3 ☐ 4 ☐
Q34   Observing other teachers in action   1 ☐ 2 ☐ 3 ☐ 4 ☐
Q35   Guided research   1 ☐ 2 ☐ 3 ☐ 4 ☐
Q36   Other forms of professional development
       which have been useful (please specify)

       In which areas of literacy teaching has your professional develop-
       ment experience been particularly useful? Tick according to the
       following: Very useful = 1; Of some use = 2; Not very useful = 3;
       I have not experienced this = 4.

Q37	Phonological awareness	1 ☐ 2 ☐ 3 ☐ 4 ☐
Q38	Knowledge of grammar	1 ☐ 2 ☐ 3 ☐ 4 ☐
Q39	Reading for information	1 ☐ 2 ☐ 3 ☐ 4 ☐
Q40	Writing purposes and forms	1 ☐ 2 ☐ 3 ☐ 4 ☐
Q41	Spelling development	1 ☐ 2 ☐ 3 ☐ 4 ☐
Q42	Reading processes	1 ☐ 2 ☐ 3 ☐ 4 ☐
Q43	Writing processes	1 ☐ 2 ☐ 3 ☐ 4 ☐
Q44	Assessment	1 ☐ 2 ☐ 3 ☐ 4 ☐
Q45	Children with literacy problems	1 ☐ 2 ☐ 3 ☐ 4 ☐
Q46	Other (please specify)	

Section 3: Your feelings about the teaching of literacy

Please read the following statements and tick the box which comes closest to your feelings about each one. Tick according to the following: Strongly agree = 1; Agree = 2; Not sure = 3; Disagree = 4; Strongly disagree = 5.

Q47   If a child says 'house' for the written word 'home', the response should be left uncorrected.   1 ☐ 2 ☐ 3 ☐ 4 ☐ 5 ☐

Q48   If children have spelt a word wrongly but their attempt is clearly logically based it should be left uncorrected.   1 ☐ 2 ☐ 3 ☐ 4 ☐ 5 ☐

Q49   It is important for a word to be repeated a number of times after it has been introduced to ensure that it will become part of a child's sight vocabulary.   1 ☐ 2 ☐ 3 ☐ 4 ☐ 5 ☐

Q50   When children do not know a word, they should be told to sound out its parts.   1 ☐ 2 ☐ 3 ☐ 4 ☐ 5 ☐

Q51   It is necessary to introduce new words before they appear in a child's reading book.   1 ☐ 2 ☐ 3 ☐ 4 ☐ 5 ☐

Q52   Fluent, accurate handwriting is the highest priority in early writing teaching.   1 ☐ 2 ☐ 3 ☐ 4 ☐ 5 ☐

Q53   In the early stages, getting children to be confident in writing is a higher priority than making sure they are accurate.   1 ☐ 2 ☐ 3 ☐ 4 ☐ 5 ☐

Q54   Most children's writing should be for audiences other than the teacher.   1 ☐ 2 ☐ 3 ☐ 4 ☐ 5 ☐

Q55　Phonic analysis (that is, breaking down a word into its sounds) is the most important form of analysis used when meeting new words.　1 ☐ 2 ☐ 3 ☐ 4 ☐ 5 ☐

Q56　It is important to correct children's spellings as they write.　1 ☐ 2 ☐ 3 ☐ 4 ☐ 5 ☐

Q57　Young writers should choose their own reasons for writing.　1 ☐ 2 ☐ 3 ☐ 4 ☐ 5 ☐

Q58　When coming to a word that is unknown, the reader should be encouraged to guess a meaning and carry on.　1 ☐ 2 ☐ 3 ☐ 4 ☐ 5 ☐

Below are listed some possible teaching activities. Alongside each, tick the box which best represents your view about the likely usefulness of the activity in teaching reading and/or writing. Tick according to the following: Strongly agree = 1; Agree = 2; Not sure = 3; Disagree = 4; Strongly disagree = 5.

Q59　Getting children to write to other children in other schools or areas of the country.　1 ☐ 2 ☐ 3 ☐ 4 ☐ 5 ☐

Q60　Teaching letter sounds as a way of helping children to build up words in reading.　1 ☐ 2 ☐ 3 ☐ 4 ☐ 5 ☐

Q61　Children listening to tape-recorded versions of stories while following the text in a book.　1 ☐ 2 ☐ 3 ☐ 4 ☐ 5 ☐

Q62　Using graded word reading schemes to structure children's introduction to reading.　1 ☐ 2 ☐ 3 ☐ 4 ☐ 5 ☐

Q63　Children completing phonic worksheets and exercises.　1 ☐ 2 ☐ 3 ☐ 4 ☐ 5 ☐

Q64　Children copying or tracing over an adult's writing.　1 ☐ 2 ☐ 3 ☐ 4 ☐ 5 ☐

Q65　Regular spelling tests using published spelling lists.　1 ☐ 2 ☐ 3 ☐ 4 ☐ 5 ☐

Q66　Using worksheets or frames to guide children's writing in particular forms.　1 ☐ 2 ☐ 3 ☐ 4 ☐ 5 ☐

Q67　Using flashcards to teach children to read words by sight.　1 ☐ 2 ☐ 3 ☐ 4 ☐ 5 ☐

Q68　Using big books with a group of children to model and share reading.　1 ☐ 2 ☐ 3 ☐ 4 ☐ 5 ☐

Q69   Children using the 'magic line'
      when writing: that is, when they
      reach a word they cannot spell,
      writing its initial sound followed by
      a line (e.g. fr—— for friendly) and
      then checking the correct spelling
      afterwards.   1 ☐ 2 ☐ 3 ☐ 4 ☐ 5 ☐
Q70   Asking children to comment upon
      and help to revise each others'
      writing.   1 ☐ 2 ☐ 3 ☐ 4 ☐ 5 ☐

Section 4: What do children need to know?

Q71–3 What do you consider to be the three most important things
      children need to learn when they first encounter reading?
Q74–6 Assuming children have attained level 2 of the National Curriculum
      in reading and are beginning Key Stage 2, what do you consider to
      be the most important things they should now learn about reading?
Q77–9 What do you consider to be the three most important things
      children need to learn when they first encounter writing?
Q80–2 Assuming children have attained level 2 of the National Curriculum
      in writing and are beginning Key Stage 2, what do you judge to be
      the most important things they should now learn about writing?

Section 5: Teaching strategies used

      Tick the reading activities which you have used in the last school
      week.
Q83   Teaching letter sounds/names   ☐
Q84   Used cloze activities   ☐
Q85   Used flashcards to teach particular words   ☐
Q86   Used sequencing activities   ☐
Q87   Read to the class   ☐
Q88   Used comprehension exercises   ☐
Q89   Used a big book with a group of children   ☐
Q90   Involved other adults in reading with children   ☐
Q91   Heard children read/read with children   ☐
Q92   Used reading scheme books   ☐
Q93   Used phonic exercises   ☐
Q94–6 List up to three other reading activities you have used in the last
      week.
      Tick the writing activities you have used in the last school week.
Q97   Letter formation/handwriting exercises   ☐
Q98   Children copying words written by the teacher   ☐
Q99   Children 'sounding out' spellings   ☐

Q100   Children doing letter string exercises   ☐
Q101   Writing news/personal views   ☐
Q102   Writing on topics chosen by children   ☐
Q103   Writing for an audience other than the teacher   ☐
Q104   Using writing frames or templates to guide writing   ☐
Q105   Writing a piece after research   ☐
Q107   Using published English materials   ☐
Q108   Interactive writing   ☐
Q109–
111   List up to three other writing activities you have used in the last week.

Section 6: Assessing children

In assessing the reading and writing of children, how often do you use each of the following approaches to assessment? Tick according to the following: I use this a great deal = 1; I use this quite often = 2; I use this sometimes = 3; I never use this = 4.

Q113	Teacher-made tests	1 ☐ 2 ☐ 3 ☐ 4 ☐
Q114	Tests from published schemes	1 ☐ 2 ☐ 3 ☐ 4 ☐
Q115	Standardised tests	1 ☐ 2 ☐ 3 ☐ 4 ☐
Q116	Marking writing products	1 ☐ 2 ☐ 3 ☐ 4 ☐
Q117	Miscue analysis	1 ☐ 2 ☐ 3 ☐ 4 ☐
Q118	Running records	1 ☐ 2 ☐ 3 ☐ 4 ☐
Q119	Observation of children	1 ☐ 2 ☐ 3 ☐ 4 ☐
Q120	SATs	1 ☐ 2 ☐ 3 ☐ 4 ☐
Q121	Children's self-assessment	1 ☐ 2 ☐ 3 ☐ 4 ☐
Q122	Other (please specify)	1 ☐ 2 ☐ 3 ☐ 4 ☐

The following reasons have been given for the assessment of children's reading and writing. Read through the list and decide which of these reasons you consider to be the most important. Write a 1 in the box next to that reason. Then select the second most important reason and write a 2 next to it. Carry on until you have ranked all of the reasons.

Q123   To monitor standards from year to year   ☐
Q124   To compare the performance of children in a class   ☐
Q125   To help in matching teaching materials to children   ☐
Q126   To diagnose children's strengths and weaknesses   ☐
Q127   To guide future teaching   ☐
Q128   To evaluate particular teaching materials   ☐

Appendix C: Interview schedules

First interview schedule

1 **Teacher details**
2 **Significant features of the session**
   What do you think was significant about the literacy teaching in that session?
   Was that what you usually do?
3 **Organisation**
   Tell me about your organisation of the literacy teaching in that session.
   How had you planned it to go?
   Did things go as you planned?
   Why did you organise the session that way?
   How did you learn to do it that way?
   What was a significant experience in learning this?
4 **Teaching strategies**
   What teaching strategies were you aware of using in the session?
   For example, how did you show children what to do?
   How did you monitor what was going on?
   Which of these strategies do you use more than others?
   Why do you use these strategies?
   How did you learn to use them?
   Were any experiences particularly influential in learning to use them?
5 **Monitoring/assessment**
   Did you make any assessments of children's learning during that session?
   How did you do that?
   How did you monitor the suitability of the activities for the children?
   How will you use the results of your monitoring/assessment?
   Can you give me any examples of how this has happened in the past?
   How did you learn to make these on-going assessments of children's learning?
   Were any experiences particularly helpful in learning this?

6 **Professional development**

What experiences have been useful to you in your professional development as a teacher of literacy?

What did these involve?

When did you undertake them?

Second interview schedule

1 **What would you say was the main content of the lesson in terms of literacy?**

What literacy content were you aiming to teach the children?

What would you like them to have learned from the lesson?

2 **Why did you choose to teach that particular content now?**

Why did you plan this lesson for today?

How does the lesson fit with your current work on literacy with this class?

How does it fit with what you think your children know already and need to know?

3 **How have you prepared the class for this lesson content?**

Have you done any other lessons involving this literacy content?

What made you think the children were ready for this content today?

4 **Was the literacy content of the lesson different for different children? If so, how?**

Did you want all the children to learn the same things?

Why did you have different aims for different children?

5 **I noticed you used the image of —— to help you teach the literacy content. Can you tell me about this?**

Why did you choose that particular image?

Have you used other images in the past?

Do you think your use of this image was successful in helping the children to understand the content?

6 **Will you follow up this lesson?**

Will you revisit this literacy content?

How will you approach it?

How will you know when to move on?

When will they next do this literacy work again?

Appendix D: The literacy quiz

In order to provide a measure of teachers' subject knowledge in literacy, they were asked during the second interview session to complete the following 'quiz'.

1 Parts of speech

In each version of the sentence below underline the required part(s) of speech.

> The experienced teacher listened patiently to her anxious pupil and then quietly guided him through the text.

a Underline the nouns
b Underline the verbs
c Underline the adjectives
d Underline the adverbs
e Underline the pronouns
f Underline the conjunction
g Underline the prepositions
h Underline the articles

2 Words

a This word has been split into syllables: mag/ni/fi/cent
  Split the following words into syllables in the same way:
      window   ready   charity
b Split the following words into phonemes in the same way:
      window   ready   charity
c Split the following words into onsets and rimes in the same way:
      cat   string   wigwam

d Each of the following words has more than one morpheme. Split them into the constituent morphemes in the same way:

export　　beautiful　　kindness

e In the following words, please ring each letter or combination of letters which you think represents a distinct sound and put the number of sounds under each word. For example: (th)(a)(t)　3

fisher　　swing　　mishap　　cough　　apple

f Words are often made of parts which convey aspects of meaning. In the following words please ring each combination of letters which conveys an aspect of meaning. For example: (walk)(ed)

running　　triangle　　playful　　oxen　　doors

3 Statements about language

Write down any reactions you have to each of the following statements:

a A verb is a doing word.
b I will always insist that the pupils who I teach follow the rules of English so that they learn to always speak and write correctly. I will make sure they always use 'shall' with 'I', that they use 'whom' when the accusative form is required, that they never split an infinitive and that they never use a preposition to end a sentence with.

4 Language variation

a Explain the difference between an accent and a dialect.
b The following is a transcript of part of the Red Riding Hood story told by a London girl whose parents originated from Jamaica.

> All of a sudden she see a wolf. The wolf say, 'Where you going little red riding hood?' She say, 'I going to my grandmother house.' 'And where you grandmother house?' 'Up on the other side of the wood.' So he say, 'OK then, little red riding hood, I go see you.' And off he run.

Describe the ways in which this girl's use of grammar differs from Standard English.

5 Children's authors

Underline the names of children's authors in the following list.

Allan Ahlberg	Helen Andrews	Nina Bawden
Arthur Ransome	Helen Cresswell	Norma Cooke
Bernard Ashley	J.R.R. Tolkein	P.E. Davies
Betsy Byars	Jan Mark	Pamela Wooley
Beverley Cleary	John Shelmadine	Pamela Yeadon
C.I. James	Judy Blume	Paul Kaiserman
C.S. Lewis	Kathleen Butterman	Penelope Lively
David Henry Wilson	lan Lawson	Peter Massey
David Taylor	Lewis Carroll	Phillippa Pearce
David Wise	Louise Rosenberg	Raymond Briggs
Dawn Glennie	Malcolm Adamson	Roald Dahl
Diana Rule	Mary Barker	Rosemary Sutcliff
Dick King-Smith	Merle Broxton	Stephanie Weinberg
Duncan Smith	Michael Kelly	Sue Townsend
Enid Blyton	Michael Rosen	Susan Edis
F.R. Smith	Myra Kersner	Terry Pratchett
Gillian Cross	Nicholas Fiske	

6 Children's reading

Teachers were asked to examine examples of two children's reading on which their miscues had been marked. Each example was followed by the child's retelling of what had been read. Teachers were asked to compare the children as readers.

The marking scheme for this part of the quiz is given below. Where teachers mentioned a feature they got one point for a mention and a further point for inferring from this to the child as a reader.

Cue use	*Identifies item*	*Infers reading behaviour*
a Number of pauses/ fluency	One child pauses more	Discussed location of pauses or reason for location
b Use of initial sound cues	Mistakes are sound correct	using initial sound cues
c Reads for understanding	The reading makes sense	Uses context cues to make sense
d Attends to syntax	The mistakes are the right part of speech	Child is using the grammar cues
e Number of words read correctly	One more correct than the other	Level of correctness in relation to the miscues
f Self-correction	Notices self-correction	Infers attempt to read for meaning
Comprehension	*What they have done*	*Infers about how reader operates*
g Sequence of events	Mentions sequence or mis-sequence	Gives possible reason, e.g. 'child understands events linked causally' or 'has read more carefully'
h Relative importance of events	Mentions the events child includes	Gives possible reason, e.g. 'child has read less carefully' or 'child has used prior knowledge'
i Degree of detail	Spots difference in detail	Gives possible reason, e.g. 'child has read less carefully'
j Prediction	Spots that one child can predict	Gives possible reason, e.g. 'child is predicting from whole story/own imagination'
k Enjoyment	Mention child's enjoyment	Give a reason for this enjoyment, e.g. 'child really understands/responds to this passage'
l Use of vocabulary from the passage	Mentions that child uses some words	Gives possible reason, e.g. 'child has read carefully and remembers what he/she has read'

7 Children's writing

Teachers were asked to compare two examples of children's writing. These had been written in response to a similar task (writing instructions), and teachers were asked to comment on the features that made each piece more or less effective as a response to the task.

The marking scheme is given below. Where teachers mentioned a feature they got one point for a general mention and a further point for a specific example.

At a sub-lexical or lexical level	General	Specific
a Spelling errors	Mention spelling errors	Of phonological, visual, aural or meaning-led types, or why made
b Breadth and appropriateness of vocabulary	Say general things such as 'uses right sort of words' or 'good vocabulary'	Give examples of appropriate vocabulary
c Use of capitalisation	Mention capitalisation	Capitalisation for sentence and names

At a sentence level	Generally	With term
d Tense	Give example	Give example and definition (e.g. in the past tense)
e Use of imperative/ declarative verbs	Give example	Give example and definition. Say which.
f Use of temporal connectives	Give example	Give example and definition
g Use of (.) and (,)	Mention punctuation	Specify full stops and commas

At a text level	Generally	With term
h Layout	Mention layout	Give alternative, e.g. sections, bullet points
i Sequential organisation	Mention organisation	Give example of order or lack of order
j Use of generic or personal participants	Example	Example and definition
k List of ingredients	Pick out ingredients in piece 1	Pick out list of ingredients and talk about its function
l Clarity and detail of the content	Mention generally	Give examples
m Reader awareness	Mention generally	Give examples
n Fitness for purpose/ genre	E.g. this is better instructions	Example and definition, e.g. it tells you how to do it and what you need

References

Adams, M.J. (1990) *Beginning to Read: Thinking and Learning About Print.* Cambridge, Mass.: MIT Press.

Adams, M.J. (1991) 'Why not phonics and whole language?' In W. Ellis (ed.) *All Language and the Creation of Literacy.* Baltimore: The Orton Dyslexia Society.

Alexander, P., Shallert, D. and Hare, V. (1991) 'Coming to terms: how researchers in learning and literacy talk about knowledge.' *Review of Educational Research* 61, 3: 265–86.

Alexander, R. (1992) *Policy and Practice in Primary Schools.* London: Routledge.

Alexander, R., Rose, J. and Woodhead, C. (1992) *Curriculum Organisation and Classroom Practice in Primary Schools.* London: HMSO.

Allington, R. (1984) 'Content coverage and contextual reading in reading groups.' *Journal of Reading Behaviour,* 16.

Ausubel, D. (1968) *Educational Psychology: A Cognitive View.* New York: Holt, Reinhart & Winston.

Barr, R. (1984) 'Beginning reading instruction: from debate to reformation.' In D. Pearson (ed.) *Handbook of Reading Research.* New York: Longman.

Basic Skills Agency (1996) *Family Literacy Works.* London: Basic Skills Agency.

Bennett, N. (1993) 'Knowledge bases for learning to teach.' In N. Bennett and C. Carré (eds) *Learning to Teach.* London: Routledge.

Bennett, N. and Dunne, E. (1992) *Managing Classroom Groups.* Hemel Hempsted: Simon & Schuster.

Bennett, N. and Turner-Bissett, R. (1993) 'Knowledge bases and teaching performance.' In N. Bennett and C. Carré (eds) *Learning To Teach.* London: Routledge.

Bennett, N., Carré, C. and Dunne, E. (1993) 'Learning to teach.' In N. Bennett and C. Carré (eds) *Learning To Teach.* London: Routledge.

Bennett, S.N., Andrae, J., Hegarty, P. and Wade, B. (1980) *Open Plan Schools: Teaching Curriculum and Design.* Slough: NFER.

Bennett, S.N., Desforges, C., Cockburn, A. and Wilkinson, B. (1984) *The Quality of Pupil Learning Experiences.* London: Lawrence Erlbaum.

Borko, W., Livingston, C., McCaleb, J. and Mauro, L. (1988) 'Student teachers' planning and post lesson reflections: patterns and implications for teacher reflection.' In J. Calderhead (ed.) *Teachers' Professional learning.* Lewes: Falmer.

Brophy, J. and Evertson, C. (1976) *Learning from Teaching: A Developmental Perspective.* Boston: Allyn & Bacon.

Brophy, J. and Good, T. (1986) 'Teacher behaviour and student achievement.' In M.C. Wittrock (ed.) *Handbook of Research In Teaching.* London: Collier Macmillan.

Bruner, J. (1986) *Actual Minds, Possible Worlds.* Cambridge, Mass.: Harvard University Press.

Cazden, C. (1992) *Whole Language Plus: Essays on Literacy in The United States and New Zealand.* New York: Teachers' College Press.

Chall, J. (1967) *Learning to Read: The Great Debate.* London: McGraw-Hill.

Clark, C., Cage, N., Marx, R., Peterson, P., Stayrook, N. and Winne, P. (1979) 'A factorial experiment on teacher structuring, soliciting, and reacting.' *Journal of Educational Psychology* 71, 4: 534–52.

Deford, D. (1985) 'Validating the construct of theoretical orientation in reading instruction.' *Reading Research Quarterly* 20: 251–367.

Denham, C. and Lieberman, A. (eds) (1980) *Time to Learn.* Washington: National Institute of Education.

Department of Education and Science (DES) (1988) *Report of the Committee of Inquiry into the Teaching of English Language.* London: HMSO.

Department of Education and Science (DES) (1995) *English in the National Curriculum.* London: HMSO.

Department for Education and Employment (DfEE) (1998) *The National Literacy Strategy: Framework for Teaching.* London: DfEE.

Downing, J. and Valtin, R. (eds) (1984) *Language Awareness and Learning to Read.* New York: Springer Verlag.

Downing, J. (1979) *Reading and Reasoning.* Edinburgh: Chambers.

Duffy, G. (1991) 'What counts in teacher education? Dilemmas in educating empowered teachers.' In J. Zutell and S. McCormack (eds) *Learner Factors/Teacher Factors: Issues in Literacy Research and Instruction: Fortieth Yearbook of the National Reading Conference.* Chicago: NRC.

Dykstra, R. (1968) 'Summary of the second grade phase of the cooperative research program in primary reading instruction.' *Reading Research Quarterly* 4: 49–70.

Flesch, R. (1955) *Why Johnny Can't Read.* New York: Harper & Row.

Foorman, B.R. (1994) 'The relevance of a connectionist model of reading for "The great debate".' *Educational Psychology Review* 6: 25–47.

Galton, M. and Simon, B. (eds) (1980) *Progress and Performance in the Primary Classroom.* London: Routledge & Kegan Paul.

Gilroy, A. and Moore, P. (1988) 'Reciprocal teaching of comprehension-fostering and comprehension-monitoring activities with ten primary school girls.' *Educational Psychology* 8, 1/2: 41–9.

Goodman, K. and Goodman, Y. (1979) 'Learning to read is natural.' In L.B. Resnik and P.A. Weaver (eds) *Theory and Practice of Early Reading.* Hillsdale, NJ: Erlbaum.

Goswami, U. and Bryant, P.E. (1990) *Phonological Skills and Learning to Read.* Hove, East Sussex: Lawrence Erlbaum.

Graham, S. and Harris, K.R. (1994) 'The effects of whole language on children's writing: a review of the literature.' *Educational Psychologist* 29: 187–92.

Grossman, P.L., Wilson, S.M. and Shulman, L.E. (1989) 'Teachers of substance: subject matter knowledge for teaching.' In M.C. Reynolds (ed.) *Knowledge Base For The Beginning Teacher.* New York: Pergamon.

Harrison, C. (1996) *Teaching Reading: What Teachers Need to Know*. Cambridge: United Kingdom Reading Association.

Harste, J. and Burke, C. (1977) 'A new hypothesis for reading teacher research: both the teaching and learning of reading are theoretically based.' In P.D. Pearson (ed.) *Reading: Theory, Research and Practice*. Clemson, SC: The National Reading Conference.

Hiebert, E.H. (1983) 'An examination of ability grouping for reading instruction.' *Reading Research Quarterly* 18: 231–55.

Hoffman, J.V. and Kugle, C. (1982) 'A study of theoretical orientation to reading and its relation to teacher verbal feedback during reading instruction.' *Journal of Classroom Interaction* 18: 2–7.

Holdaway, D. (1979) *The Foundations of Literacy*. Auckland: Ashton Scholastic.

Hook, C.M. and Rosenshine, B.U. (1979) 'Accuracy of teacher reports of their classroom behaviour.' *Review of Educational Research* 49: 1–12.

Kavanagh, J. and Mattingley, I. (eds) (1972) *Language by Ear and by Eye*. Cambridge, Mass.: MIT Press.

Leinhardt, G. and Greeno, J. (1986) 'The cognitive skill of teaching.' *Journal of Educational Psychology* 78: 75–95.

Mather, N. (1992) 'Whole language reading instruction for students with learning abilities; caught in the crossfire.' *Learning Disabilities Research and Practice* 7: 87–95.

Moore, P. (1988) 'Reciprocal teaching and reading comprehension: a review.' *Journal of Research in Reading* 11, 1: 3–14.

Morrow, L.M. (1990) 'Preparing the classroom environment to promote literacy during play.' *Early Childhood Research Quarterly* 5: 537–54.

Morrow, L.M. (1991) 'Relationships among physical design of play centres, teachers' emphasis on literacy play, and children's behaviours during play.' In J. Zutell and S. McCormack (eds) *Learner Factors/Teacher Factors: Issues in Literacy Research and Instruction: Fortieth Yearbook of the National Reading Conference*. Chicago: NRC.

Morrow, L.M. (1992) 'The impact of literature based programmes on literacy achievement, use of literature and attitudes of children from ethnic minority backgrounds.' *Reading Research Quarterly* 27: 251–75.

Mortimore, P., Sammons, P., Stoll, L., Lewis, D. and Ecob, R. (1988) *School Matters*. Wells, Somerset: Open Books.

Munby, H. (1984) 'A qualitative study of teachers' beliefs and principles.' *Journal of Research in Science Teaching* 21: 27–38.

National Literacy Project (1997) *The Framework of Teaching Objectives*. Unpublished draft document, National Literacy Project.

Nespor, J. (1987) 'The role of beliefs in the practice of teaching.' *Journal of Curriculum Studies* 19: 317–28.

Neuman, S.B. and Roskos, K. (1990) 'The influence of literacy enriched play settings on pre-schoolers engagement with written language.' In J. Zutell and S. McCormack (eds) *Literacy Theory and Research: Analyses from Multiple Paradigms*. Chicago: NRC.

Neuman, S.B. and Roskos, K. (1992) 'Literacy objects as cultural tools: effects on children's literacy behaviours at play.' *Reading Research Quarterly* 27: 203–25.

Office for Standards in Education (OFSTED) (1996) *World's Apart? A Review of International Surveys of Educational Achievement Involving England.* London: Office for Standards in Education.

Palincsar, A.S. and Brown, A.L. (1984) 'Reciprocal teaching of comprehension fostering and comprehension monitoring strategies.' *Cognition and Instruction* 1: 117–57.

Poulson, L., Radnor, H. and Turner-Bissett, R. (1996) 'From policy to practice: language education, English teaching and curriculum reform in secondary schools in England.' *Language in Education* 10, 1: 33–46.

Powell, M. (1980) 'The beginning teacher education study: a brief history of a major research project.' In C. Denham and A. Lieberman (eds) *Time to Learn.* Washington: National Institute of Education.

Pressley, M. and Rankin, J. (1994) 'More about whole language methods of reading instruction for students at risk for early reading failure.' *Learning Disabilities Research and Practice* 9: 156–67.

Pressley, M., Rankin, J. and Yokoi, L. (1996) 'A survey of instructional practices of primary teachers nominated as effective in promoting literacy.' *Elementary School Journal* 96, 4: 363–84.

Pressley, M., Gaskins, I., Cunicelli, E.A., Burdick, N.J., Schaub-Matt, M., Lee, D.S. and Powell, N. (1991) 'Strategy instruction at Benchmark School: a faculty interview study.' *Learning Disability Quarterly* 14: 19–48.

Pressley, M., El-Dinary, P.B., Gaskins, I., Schuder, T., Bergman, J., Almasai, L. and Brown, R. (1992) 'Beyond direct explanation: transactional instruction of reading comprehension strategies.' *Elementary School Journal* 92: 511–54.

Raban, B. (1991) 'The role of schooling in initial literacy.' *Educational and Child Psychology* 8, 3: 41–59.

Richardson, V. (ed.) (1994) *Teacher Change and the Staff Development Process.* New York: Teachers' College Press.

Rose, J. (1996) 'What our schools must teach.' *The Times*, 8th May.

Rosenshine, B.V. (1979) 'Content, time and direct instruction.' In P. Peterson and H. Walburg (eds) *Research on Teaching; Concepts, Findings and Implications.* Berkeley, Calif.: McCutchan.

Rumelhart, D. (1980) 'Schemata: the building blocks of cognition.' In R. Spiro, B. Bruce and W. Brewer (eds) *Theoretical Issues In Reading Comprehension.* Hillsdale, NJ: Lawrence Erlbaum.

Samson, G.E., Strykowski, B., Weinstein, T. and Walburg, H.J. (1987) 'The effects of teacher questioning on student achievement.' *Journal of Educational Research* 80, 5: 290–5.

Shulman, L.S. (1986) 'Those who understand: knowledge growth in teaching.' *Educational Researcher* 15, 2: 8–9.

Shulman, L.S. (1987) 'Knowledge and teaching: foundations of the new reform.' *Harvard Educational Review* 57, 1: 1–22.

Silcock, P. (1993) 'Can we teach effective teaching?' *Educational Review* 45, 1: 13–19.

Smith, L. and Land, M. (1981) 'Low-inference verbal behaviors related to teacher clarity.' *Journal of Classroom Interaction* 17, 1: 37–42.

Stahl, S.A. and Miller, P.D. (1989) 'Whole language and language experience approaches for beginning reading: a quantitative research synthesis.' *Review of Educational Research* 59: 87–116.

Stahl, S.A., McKenna, M.C. and Pagnucco, J.R. (1994) 'The effects of whole language instruction: an update and reappraisal.' *Educational Psychologist* 29: 175–86.

Stainthorp, R. (1996) 'A children's author recognition test: a useful tool in reading research.' *Journal of Research in Reading* 17: 2.

Stallings, J., Cory, R., Fairweather, J. and Needles, M. (1977) *Early Childhood Classroom Evaluation*. Menlo Park, Calif.: SRI International.

Stallings, J., Cory, R., Fairweather, J. and Needles, M. (1978) *A Study of Basic Reading Skills Taught In Secondary Schools*. Menlo Park, CA: SRI International.

Stanovich, K.E. (1986) 'Matthew effects in reading: some consequences of individual differences in reading in the acquisition of literacy.' *Reading Research Quarterly* 21: 360–406.

Taylor, D. (1983) *Family Literacy*. Portsmouth, NH: Heinemann.

Tobin, K. and Capie, W. (1982) 'Relationships between classroom process variables and middle school science achievement.' *Journal of Educational Psychology* 74, 3: 441–54.

Weaver, C. (1990) *Understanding Whole Language: From Principles to Practice*. Portsmouth, NH: Heinemann.

Webster, A., Beveridge, M. and Reed, M. (1996) *Managing the Literacy Curriculum*. London: Routledge.

Westerhof, K.J. (1992) 'On the effectiveness of teaching: direct versus indirect instruction.' *School Effectiveness and School Improvement* 3, 3: 204–15.

Wood, D.J. (1988) *How Children Think and Learn*. Oxford: Blackwell.

Wragg, E.C. (1984) *Classroom Teaching Skills*. London: Croom Helm.

Wray, D. and Lewis, M. (1994) 'Extending literacy in the junior school: a curriculum development project.' In A. Littlefair (ed.) *Literacy for Life*. United Kingdom Reading Association.

Wray, D. and Lewis, M. (1997) *Extending Literacy: Children Reading and Writing Non-Fiction*. London: Routledge.

Wray, D. (1993) 'Involving student teachers in teaching children with reading problems.' *Journal of Education for Teaching* 19, 2: 293–302.

Wray, D. and Medwell, J. (1994) 'Student teachers and teaching reading.' *Reading* 28, 3: 43–5.

Index